The Prep and Cook Handbook

Mastering the Basics

By

Gerard A. Coleman

I.

HEALTH, ECONOMY, AND PLEASURE, IN FOOD.

The following are the special advantages of the following pages:

The directions for preparing and cooking food provide a large variety of articles which, according to all medical and physiological rules, are *healthful*.

There is also a good variety of dishes which are *economical*.

There are unusual contrivances for saving *time* and *labor* in cooking, having special reference to women of culture in new settlements, who have few conveniences, poor markets, and either poor servants or none at all.

As the relish of food depends chiefly on the proper *seasonings* and *flavors*, there are more specific methods given than the ordinary rule, "season to the taste," which leaves all to the judgment of the careless or the ignorant.

The recipes are put in *short and clear language*, so as to be easily read and understood by servants, and also more readily remembered.

These recipes and directions have been criticised and tested by some of the best housekeepers of all sections of the nation.

RULES OF HEALTH IN REGARD TO FOOD AND DRINK.

Always eat slowly and chew very thoroughly, as this greatly aids digestion.

Do not eat between meals, because this mixes the partly digested food with the new supply, and impedes digestion. Meals should be about five hours apart, to give the stomach time to rest after the labor of the muscles in digestion.

Do not eat too much, as this tends to indigestion and taxes the organs that must labor to throw off the excess. A healthful appetite is a safe guide, if meals are at regular and proper periods, the food simple, and nothing is taken after hunger is satisfied. *Successive* dishes of food are unwise for children and invalids, tempting them to eat too much. Children should have the kind of food they like best, if it is healthful, and should make their whole meal of it. Soups, and then meats, and then tempting desserts, are very dangerous to the young and the delicate, who have formed no habits of self-control, or are ignorant of their dangers.

Do not require children to eat what they do not relish, as it is proved by many experiments that food which is relished is better digested and more healthful than that which is not. This shows the importance of care in seasoning food properly, and of rules to aid in so doing.

Do not multiply dishes for one meal, but rather have a variety at successive meals; for digestion is easier and more perfect when there are but few articles taken at one meal, and grows more difficult as the variety increases.

Food and drinks should not be very hot, as this tends to destroy the teeth.

Drink moderately while eating—one tumbler or tea-cupful only. If thirsty, drink freely before eating.

Do not drink very cold water or take ices after a full meal, as cooling the stomach lessens the power of digestion.

Do not drink tea or coffee, except when so largely diluted as not to stimulate. It will be found that a *gradual* diminution of strength in these drinks will modify one's taste, so that after a few months, weak dilutions will be relished as much as strong. An expert housekeeper can change dangerous habits in this way with little trouble, and sometimes without notice by those benefited.

Be careful to have *pure* water to drink, as most important to health. If water is impure, filter it through sand and powdered charcoal. The free drinking of *pure*, cold water before meals is healthful, tending to purify the blood, strengthen the stomach, and thus promoting digestion.

In using salt and pepper, diversities of strength make a difficulty in giving very exact directions; so also do inequalities in the size of spoons and tumblers. But so much can be done that a housekeeper, after one trial, can give exact directions to her cook, or with a pencil alter the recipe.

It is a great convenience to have recipes that employ measures which all families have on hand, so as not to use steel-yards and balances. The following will be found the most convenient:

A medium size tea-spoon, even full, equals 60 drops or one eighth of an ounce.

A medium size table-spoon, even full, equals two tea-spoonfuls.

One ounce equals eight even tea-spoonfuls, or four table-spoonfuls.

One gill equals eight even table-spoonfuls.

Half a gill equals four even table-spoonfuls.

Two gills equal half a pint, and four gills equal one pint.

One common size tumbler equals half a pint, or two gills.

One pint equals two tumblerfuls, or four gills.

One quart equals four tumblerfuls, or eight gills.

Four quarts equal one gallon.

Four gallons equal one peck.

Four pecks equal one bushel.

A quart of sifted flour, heaped, a sifted quart of sugar, and a softened quart of butter each weigh about a pound, and so nearly that measuring is as good as weighing.

Water is heavier, and a pint of water weighs nearly a pound.

Ten eggs weigh about one pound

II.

MARKETING AND THE CARE OF MEATS.

Every young woman, at some period of her life, may need the instructions of this chapter. Thousands will have the immediate care of buying meats for the family; and even those who are not themselves obliged to go to market, should have the knowledge which will enable them to direct their servants what and how to buy, and to judge whether the household, under their management, is properly served or not. Nothing so thoroughly insures the intelligent obedience of orders, as evidence that the person ordering knows exactly what is wanted.

The directions given in this and the ensuing chapters on meats, were carefully written, first in Cincinnati, with the counsel and advice of business men practically engaged in such matters. They have been recently rewritten in Hartford, Conn., after consultation with intelligent butchers and grocers.

MARKETING.

BEEF.

The animal, when slaughtered, should be bled very thoroughly. The care taken by the Jews in this and other points draws custom from other sects to their markets. The skin is tanned for leather, and the fat is used for candles and other purposes. The tail is used for soups, and the liver, heart, and tripe are also used for cooking. The body is split into two parts, through the back-bone, and each half is divided as marked in the drawing above. There are diverse modes of cutting and naming the parts, butchers in New-England, in New-York, in the South, and in the West, all making some slight differences; but the following is the most common method.

1. The *head:* frequently used for mince-pies; sometimes it is tried up for oil, and then the bones are used for fertilizers. The horns are used to make buttons and combs, and various other things. 2. The *neck;* used for soups and stews. 3. The *chuck-rib,* or *shoulder,* having four ribs. It is used for corning, stews, and soup, and some say the best steaks are from this piece. 4. The *front of the shoulder,* or the *shoulder-clod,* which is sometimes called the *brisket.* 5. The *back of the shoulder;* used for corning, soups, and stews. 6. The *fore-shin,* or *leg;* used for soups. 7, 7. The *plate-pieces;* the front one is called the brisket, (as is also 4,) and is used for corning, soups, and stews. The back plate-piece is called the *flank,* and is divided into the *thick flank,* or upper *sirloin,* and the *lower flank.* These are for roasting and corning. 8. The *standing ribs,* divided into *first, second,* and *third cuts;* used for roasting. The second cut is the best of the three. 9. The *sirloin,* which is the best roasting piece. 10. The *sirloin steak* and the *porter-house steak;* used for broiling. 11. The *rump,* or *aitch-bone;* used for soup or corning, or to cook *à la mode.* 12. The *round,* or *buttock;* used for corning, or for *à la mode;* also for dried beef. 13. The *hock,* or *hind shank;* used for soups.

In selecting *Beef,* choose that which has a loose grain, easily yielding to pressure, of a clear red, with whitish fat. If the lean is purplish, and the fat yellow, it is poor beef. Beef long kept turns a darker color than fresh killed. Stall-fed beef has a lighter color than grass-fed.

Ox beef is the best, and next, that of a heifer.

In cold weather, it is economical to buy a hind quarter; have it cut up, and what is not wanted immediately, pack with snow in a barrel. All meats grow tender by keeping. Do not let meats freeze; if they do, thaw them in cold water, and do not cook it till fully thawed. A piece weighing ten pounds requires ten or twelve hours to thaw.

VEAL.

The calf should not be slaughtered until it is six weeks old. Spring is the best time for veal. It is divided as marked in the drawing.

1. The *head*, sold with the *pluck*, which includes the *heart, liver*, and *sweet-breads*. 2. The *rack*, including the neck; used for stews, pot-pies, and broths; also for chops and roasting. 3. The *shoulder*. This, and also half the rack and ribs of the fore-quarter, are sometimes roasted, and sometimes used for stews, broths, and cutlets. 4. The *fore-shank*, or *knuckle*; used for broths. 5. The *breast;* used for stews and soups; also to stuff and bake. 6. The *loin;* used for roasting. 7. The *fillet*, or *leg*, including the hind flank; used for cutlets, or to stuff and boil, or to stuff and roast, or bake. 8. The *hind shank*, or *hock*, or *knuckle;* used for soups. *The feet* used for jelly.

In selecting *Veal*, take that which is firm and dry, and the joints stiff, having the lean a delicate red, the kidney covered with fat, and the fat very white. If you buy the head, see that the eyes are plump and lively, and not dull and sunk in the head. If you buy the legs, get those which are not skinned, as the skin is good for jelly or soup.

MUTTON

1. The *shoulder;* for boiling or corning. 2, 2. The *neck* and *rack;* for boiling or corning. 3. The *loin;* is roasted, or broiled as chops. 4. The *leg;* is boiled, or broiled, or staffed and roasted. Many salt and smoke the leg, and call it smoked venison. 5. The *breast;* for boiling or corning.

In choosing *Mutton*, take that which is bright red and close-grained, with firm and white fat. The meat should feel tender and springy on pressure. Notice the vein on the neck of the fore-quarter, which should be a fine blue.

PORK.

1. The *leg*, or *ham;* used for smoking. 2. The *hind loin*. 3. The *fore loin*. 4. The *spare-rib;* for roasting; sometimes including all the ribs. 5. The *hand*, or *shoulder*; sometimes smoked, and sometimes corned and boiled. 6. The *belly*, or *spring*, for corning or salting down. The *feet* are used for jelly, head-cheese, and souse.

In selecting *Pork*, if young, the lean can be easily broken when pinched, and the skin can be indented by nipping with the fingers. The fat also will be white and soft. *Thin* rind is beat.

In selecting *Hams*, run a knife along the bone, and if it comes out clean, the ham is good; but if it comes out smeared, it is spoiled. Good bacon has white fat, and the lean adheres closely to the bone. If the bacon has yellow streaks, it is rusty, and not fit to use.

In selecting *Poultry*, choose those that are full grown, but not old. When young and fresh-killed, the skin is thin and tender, the joints not very stiff, and the eyes full and bright. The breast-bone shows the age, as it easily yields to pressure if young, and is tough when old. If young, you can with a pin easily tear the skin. A goose, when old, has red and hairy legs; but when young, they are yellow, and have few hairs. The pin-feathers are the roots of feathers, which break off and remain in the skin, and always indicate a *young* bird. When very neatly dressed, they are pulled out.

Poultry and birds ought to be killed by having the head cut off, and then hung up by the legs to bleed freely. This makes the flesh white and more healthful.

In selecting *Fish*, take those that are firm and thick, having stiff fins and bright scales, the gills bright red, and the eyes full and prominent. When fish are long out of water, they grow soft, the fins bend easily, the scales are dim, the gills grow dark, and the eyes sink and shrink away. Be sure and have them dressed immediately; sprinkle them with salt, and use them, if possible, the same day. In warm weather, put them in ice, or corning, for the next day.

Shell-fish can be decided upon only by the smell. Lobsters are not good unless alive, or else boiled before offered for sale. They are black when alive, and red when boiled. When to be boiled, they are to be put alive into boiling water, which is the quickest and least cruel way to end their life.

THE CARE OF MEATS.

In hot weather, if there is no refrigerator, then wipe meat dry, sprinkle on a little salt and pepper, and hang in the cellar. Or, still better, wrap it, thus prepared, in a dry cloth, and cover it with charcoal or with wood-ashes. Mutton, wrapped in a cloth wet with vinegar, and, laid on the ground of a *dry* cellar, keeps well and improves in tenderness.

Hang meat a day or two after it is killed before corning it.

In winter, meat is kept finely if well packed in snow, without salting; but some say it lessens the sweetness.

Frozen meat must be thawed in cold water, and not cooked till entirely thawed.

Beef and mutton are improved by keeping as long as they remain sweet. If meat begins to taint, wash it and rub it with powdered charcoal, which it often removes the taint. Sometimes rubbing with salt will cure it. Soda water is good also.

Take all the kernels out that you will find in the round, and thick end of the flank of beef, and in the fat, and fill the holes with salt. This will preserve it longer.

Salt your meat, in summer, as soon as you receive it.

A pound and a half of salt rubbed into twenty-five pounds of beef, will corn it so as to last several days in ordinary warm weather; or put it in strong brine.

In most books of recipes there are several different ones for corning, for curing pork hams, and for other uses, while an in experienced person is at a loss to know which is best. The recipes here given are decided to be *the best*, after an examination of quite a variety, by the writer, who has resided where they were used; and she knows that the very best results are secured by these directions. These also are pronounced the best by business men of large experience.

To Salt down Beef to keep the Year round.—One hundred pounds of beef; four quarts of rock-salt, pounded fine; four ounces of saltpetre, pounded fine; four pounds of brown sugar. Mix well. Put a layer of meat on the bottom of the barrel, with a thin layer of this mixture under it. Pack the meat in layers, and between each put equal proportions of this mixture, allowing a little more to the top layers. Then pour in brine till the barrel is full.

To cleanse Calf's Head and Feet.—Wash clean, and sprinkle pounded resin over the hair; dip in boiling water and take out immediately, and then scrape them clean; then soak them in water for four days, changing the water every day.

To prepare Rennet.—Take the stomach of a new-killed calf, and do not wash it, as it weakens the gastric juice. Hang it in a cool and dry place five days or so; then turn the inside out, and slip off the curds with the hand. Then fill it with salt, with a little saltpetre mixed in, and lay it in a stone pot, pouring on a tea-spoonful of vinegar, and sprinkling on a handful of salt. Cover it closely, and keep for use. After six weeks, take a piece four inches square and put it in a bottle with five gills of cold water and two gills of rose brandy; stop it close, and shake it when you use it. A table-spoonful is enough for a quart of milk.

To salt down Fish.—Scale, cut off the heads, open down the back, and remove most of the spine, to have them keep better. Lay them in salt water two hours, to extract blood. Sprinkle with fine salt, and let them lie over night. Then mix one peck of coarse and fine salt, one ounce of saltpetre, (or half an ounce of saltpetre and half an ounce of saleratus,) and one pound of sugar. Then pack in a firkin. Begin with a layer of salt, then a layer of fish, skin downward. A peck of salt will answer for twenty-five shad, and other fish in proportion.

As in most country families, when meat is salted for the year's use, pork is the meat most generally and most largely relied upon, considerable space is devoted to its proper preparation. Special attention is given to various modes of curing and preserving it.

To try out Lard.—Take what is called *the leaves*, and take off all the skin, cut it into pieces an inch square, put it into a clean pot over a slow fire, and try it till the scraps look a reddish-brown, taking great care not to let it burn, which would spoil the whole. Then strain it through a, strong cloth, into a stone pot, and set it away for use.

Take the fat to which the smaller intestines are attached, (not the large ones,) and the flabby pieces of pork not fit for salting, try these in the same way, and set the fat thus obtained where it will freeze, and by spring the strong taste will be gone, and then it can be used for frying. A tea-cup of water prevents burning while trying.

Corn-fed pork is best. Pork made by still-house slops is almost poisonous, and hogs that live on offal never furnish healthful food. If hogs are properly fed, the pork is not unhealthful.

Pork with kernels in it is measly, and is unwholesome.

A thick skin shows that the pork is old, and that it requires more time to boil. If bought pork is very salt, soak it some hours. Do not let pork freeze, if you intend to salt it.

The gentleman who uses the following recipe for curing pork hams, says it has these advantages over all others he has tried or heard of, namely, the hams thus cured are sweeter than by any other method; they are more solid and tender, and are cured in less than half the time. Moreover, they do not attract flies so much as other methods:

Recipe for Molasses-cured Hams.—Moisten every part of the ham with molasses, and then for every hundred pounds use one quart of fine salt and four ounces of saltpetre, rubbing them in very thoroughly at every point. Put the hams thus prepared in a tight cask for four days. Then rub again with molasses and one quart of salt, and return the hams to the cask for four days. Repeat this the third and the fourth time, and then smoke the hams. This process takes only sixteen days, while other methods require five or six weeks.

The following is the best recipe for the ordinary mode of curing hams; and the brine or pickle thus prepared is equally good for corning and all other purposes for which brine is used. Some persons use saleratus instead of the saltpetre, and others use half and half of each, and say it is an improvement:

Brine or Pickle for corning Hams, Beef, Fork, and Hung Beef.—Four gallons of water; two pounds of rock-salt, and a, little more of common salt; two ounces of saltpetre; one quart of molasses. Mix, but do not boil. Put the hams in a barrel and pour this over them, and keep them covered with it for six weeks. If more brine is needed, make it in the same proportions.

Brine for Beef, Pork, Tongues, and Hung Beef.—Four gallons of water; one and a half pounds of sugar; one ounce of saltpetre; one ounce of saleratus. Add salt; and if it is for use only a month or two, use six pounds of salt; if for all the year, use *nine* pounds. In hot weather, rub the meat with salt before putting it in, and let it lie for three hours, to extract the blood. When tongues and hung beef are taken out, wash the pieces, and, when smoked, put them in paper bags, and hang in a dry place.

Brine by Measure, easily made.—One gallon of cold water; one quart of rock-salt, and two of blown salt; one heaping table-spoonful of saltpetre, (or half as much of saleratus, with half a table-spoonful of saltpetre;) six heaping table-spoonfuls of brown sugar. Mix, but not boil. Keep it as long as salt remains undissolved at bottom. When scum rises, add more salt, sugar, saltpetre, and soda.

To salt down Pork.—Allow peck of salt for sixty pounds. Cover the bottom of the barrel with salt an inch deep. Put down one layer of pork, and cover that with salt half an inch thick. Continue thus till the barrel is full. Then pour in as much strong brine as the barrel will receive. Keep coarse salt between all pieces, so that the brine can circulate. When a, white scum or bloody-looking matter rises on the top, scald the brine and add more salt. Leave out bloody and lean pieces for sausages. Pack as tight as possible, the rind next the barrel; and let it be *always* kept *under* the brine. Some use a stone for this purpose. In salting down a new supply, take the old brine, boil it down and remove all the scum, and then use it to pour over the pork. The pork may be used in six weeks after salting.

To prepare Cases for Sausages.—Empty the cases, taking care not to tear them. Wash them thoroughly, and cut into lengths of two yards each. Then take a candle-rod, and fastening one end of a case to the top of it, turn the case inside outward. When all are turned, wash very thoroughly, and scrape them with a scraper made for the purpose, keeping them in warm water till ready to scrape. Throw them into salt and water to soak till used. It is a very difficult job to scrape them clean without tearing them. When finished, they look transparent and very thin.

Sausage-Meat.—Take one third fat and two thirds lean pork, and chop it; and then to every twelve pounds of meat add twelve large even spoonfuls of pounded salt, nine of sifted sage, and six of sifted black pepper. Some like a little summer-savory. Keep it in a cool and dry place.

Another Recipe.—To twenty-five pounds of chopped meat, which should be one third fat and two thirds lean, put twenty spoonfuls of sage, twenty-five of salt, ten of pepper, and four of summer-savory.

Bologna Sausages.—Take equal portions of veal, pork, and ham; chop them fine; season with sweet herbs *and* pepper; put them in cases; boil them till tender, and then dry them.

To Smoke Hams.—Make a small building of boards, nailing strips over the cracks to confine the smoke. Have within cross-sticks, on which to hang the hams. Have only one opening at top, at the end furthest from the fire. Set it up so high that a small stove can be set under or very near it, with the smoke-pipe entering the floor at the opposite end from the slide. These directions are for a wooden house, and it is better thus than to have a fire *within* a brick house, because too much warmth lessens the flavor and tenderness of the hams. Change the position of the hams once or twice, then all are treated alike. When this cannot be done, use an inverted barrel or hogshead, with a hole for the smoke to escape, and resting on stones; and keep a small, smouldering fire. Cobs are best, as giving a better flavor; and brands or chips of walnut wood are next best. Keeping a small fire a longer time is better than quicker smoking, as too much heat gives the hams a strong taste, and they are less sweet.

The house and barrel are shown in Fig. 75, which follows:

Fig. 75.

III.

STEWS AND SOUPS.

The most economical modes of cooking, as to *time, care,* and *labor,* are stews, soups, and hashes; and when properly seasoned, they are great favorites, especially with children.

Below is a drawing of a stew and soup-kettle that any tinman can easily make. Its advantages are that, after the meat is put in, there is no danger of scorching, and no watching is required, except to keep up the fire aright, so as to have a steady simmering. Another advantage is that, by the tight cover, the steam and flavors are confined, and the cooking thus improved. Then, in taking up the stew, it offers several conveniences, as will be found on trial.

Fig. 76.

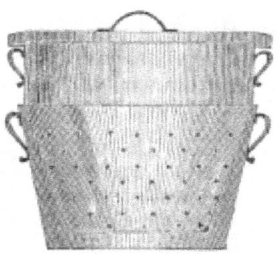

This stew-kettle consists of two pans, the inner one not fastened but fitting tight to the outer, with holes the size of a large pin-head commencing half an inch from the bottom and continuing to within two inches of the top of the under pan. It has a flat lid, on which may be placed a weight, to confine steam and flavors. The holes may be an inch apart. The size of the kettle must depend on the size of the family; it may be of any desired size.

GENERAL DIRECTIONS.

Generally, in making stews, use soft water; but when only hard is at hand, put in half a tea-spoonful of soda to every two quarts of water. Put in all the bones and gristle first, breaking the bones thoroughly.

Rub fresh meat with salt, and put it in *cold* water, for soups, as this extracts the juices.

As soon as water begins to boil, skim repeatedly till no more scum rises. Never let water boil hard for soups or stews; for

> "Meat fast boiled.
> Is meat half spoiled."

Let the water *simmer gently* and not stop simmering long, as this injures both looks and flavor.

Keep in water enough to cover the meat, or it becomes hard and dark.

In preparing for soups, it is best to make a good deal of broth at one time; cool it slowly, first removing sediment by straining through a colander. When cold, remove the fat from the top, and keep the liquor for soups and gravies. This is called *stock*, and as such should have no other seasoning than salt. The other seasoning is to be put in when heated and combined with other material for soup.

In hot weather, stock will keep only a day or two; but in cool weather, three or four days. If vegetables were boiled in it, it will turn sour sooner.

Remnants of cooked meats may be used together for soup; but take care that none is tainted, thus spoiling all. Liquor in which corned beef is boiled should be saved to mix with stock of fresh meat, and then little or no salt is needed. The recipes for stews that follow will make good soups by adding more water.

Beef and Potato Stew.—Cut up four pounds of beef into strips three inches by two, and put them into two quarts of water, with one onion sliced very fine. Let this *simmer* four hours. Add in half a cup of warm water six even tea-spoonfuls of salt, three of sugar, three of vinegar, a tea-spoonful of black pepper, and six heaping tea-spoonfuls of flour, lumps rubbed out. Pour these upon the meat; cut up, slice, and add six potatoes, and let all stew till the meat is very tender, and the potatoes are soft. If potatoes are omitted, leave out half a tea-spoonful of salt and a pinch of the pepper.

Be sure and skim very thoroughly when boiling commences, and do not allow hard boiling, but only a gentle simmer.

French Mutton and Turnip Stew.—Cut up two pounds of mutton, with a little of the fat, into two-inch squares. Rub two heaping table-spoonfuls of butter into two table-spoonfuls of flour, and stir it into the meat, with water just enough to cover it. Add three *even* tea-spoonfuls of salt, half a one of pepper, four of sugar, a sprig of parsley, and a small onion, sliced very fine. Skim as soon as it begins to boil, and then add thirty pieces of turnips, each an inch square, that have been fried brown. Let all stew till meat and turnips are tender; throw out the parsley, and serve with the turnips in the centre, and the meat around it.

A Simple Mutton Stew.—Cut four pounds of mutton into two-inch squares, add four *even* tea-spoonfuls of salt, four of sugar, half a one of pepper, and a small onion, sliced fine. Stew three hours, and then thicken with five tea-spoonfuls of flour, lumps rubbed out. Six tomatoes, or some tomato catsup, improves this.

A Beel Stew, with Vegetable Flavors.—Cut up four pounds of beef into two-inch squares, and add two quarts of water. Let it stew one hour. Then add one sliced onion, two sliced turnips, two sliced carrots, four sliced tomatoes, four heaping tea-spoonfuls of salt, one small tea-spoonful of pepper, four tea-spoonfuls of sugar, and five cloves. Let it stew till there is only about a tea-cupful of gravy, and thicken this with a little flour.

The above may be cooked without cutting up the meat, and it is good eaten cold. Pressing it under a weight improves it, and so does putting it an oven for half an hour.

A Stew of Chicken, Duck, or Turkey, with Celery or Tomatoes.— Take a quart of lukewarm water, and add two heaping tea-spoonfuls of salt, two of sugar, and a salt-spoonful of pepper. Cut up a large head of celery, or four large tomatoes. Cut the fowl into eight or more pieces, and let all simmer together two hours, or till the meat is very tender. Then add two table-spoonfuls of butter, worked into as much flour, and let it simmer fifteen minutes.

A Favorite Irish Stew.—Cut two pounds of mutton into pieces two inches square; add a little of the chopped fat, three tea-spoonfuls of salt, half a one of black pepper, two of sugar, two sliced onions, and a quart of water. Let them simmer half an hour, and then add six peeled potatoes, cut in quarters, that have soaked in cold water an hour. Let the whole stew an hour longer, or rather till the meat is very tender. Skim it at first and just before taking up.

Veal Stew.—Put a knuckle of veal into two quarts of boiling water, with three tea-spoonfuls of salt and half a tea-spoonful of ground pepper. Then chop fine and tie in muslin rag one carrot, two small onions, a small bunch of summer-savory, and another of parsley; put them in the water, and let them stew three or four hours, till the meat is very tender. There should only be about half a, pint of gravy at the bottom. Pour in *boiling* water, if needed. Strain the gravy, and thicken with four spoonfuls of flour or potato-starch, and let it boil up a minute only. This is improved by adding at first half a pound of salt pork or ham, cut in strips. When this is done, no salt is to be used, or only one tea-spoonful. Tomatoes improve it.

Another.—Cut four pounds of veal into strips one inch thick and three inches long, and peel and soak eight potatoes cut into slices half an inch thick. Then put a layer of veal at the bottom, and alternate layers of potatoes and veal, with a layer of salt pork on the top. Put four tea-spoonfuls of salt, half a one of pepper, four of sugar, and six tea-spoonfuls of flour, with lumps rubbed out, into two quarts of water. Pour all upon the veal and potatoes, and let them stew till the veal is very tender. Celery or tomatoes will improve this.

A Favorite Turkish Stew, (called Pilaff.)—Take some rich broth, seasoned to the taste with pepper, salt, and tomato catsup. Add two tea-cups of rice, and let it simmer till the rice absorbs as much as it will take up without losing its form—say about fifteen minutes. Cut up a chicken, and season it with salt and pepper, and fry it in sweet butter or cream. Then put the chicken in the centre of the rice, and cover it entirely with rice. Then pour on half a pound of melted butter, and let it stand where it is hot, and yet will not fry, for fifteen minutes. To be served hot.

A Rice or Hominy Stew.—Take four pounds of any kind of fresh meat, cut into pieces two inches square, and put in the stew-pan with one pint of hominy. Then put into two quarts of warm water five heaping tea-spoonfuls of salt, four of sugar, half a one of pepper, and three of vinegar. Let them simmer four or five hours, till the meat is very tender. A tea-cup of rice may be used instead of hominy. A little salt pork improves this, as well as all other stews.

A Favorite English Beef Stew.—Simmer a shank or hock of beef, in four quarts of water, with four heaping table-spoonfuls of salt, until the beef is soft and the water reduced to about two quarts. Then add peeled and soaked potatoes cut into thick slices, two tea-spoonfuls of pepper, two of sweet marjoram, and two of either thyme or summer savory. Stew till the potatoes are soft, add bread-crumbs and more salt if needful. One or two onions cut fine, and put in at first, improve it for most persons.

French Stew, or Pot au Feu.—Put three pounds of fresh meat into three quarts of cold water, with two tea-spoonfuls of salt. When it begins to simmer, add a gill of cold water, and skim thoroughly. Then add a quarter of a pound of liver, a medium-sized carrot sliced, two small turnips, two middle-sized leeks, half a head of celery, one sprig of parsley, a bay leaf, one onion with two cloves stuck in it, and two cloves of garlic. Simmer five hours. Strain the broth into a soup-dish, and serve the meat and vegetables on a platter. If more water is needed, add that which is boiling.

When the dish is served all together, it is called *Pot au Feu,* and the vessel in which it is cooked has the same name. It is the common dish of the French peasantry.

The following is the recipe for the favorite Spanish dish. A superior housekeeper tried it, and it was so much liked that several of her family were harmed *by eating too much:*

Spanish olla, Podrida.—Fry four ounces of salt pork in the pot, and, when partly done, add two pounds of fresh beef and a quarter of a pound of ham. Add two tea-spoonfuls of salt in cold water, and only enough just to cover the meat. Skim carefully the first half-hour, and then add a gill of peas, (if dried, soak them an hour first,) half a head of cabbage, one carrot, one turnip, two leeks, three stalks of celery, three stalks of parsley, two stalks of thyme, two cloves, two onions sliced, two cloves of garlic, ten pepper-corns, and a pinch of powdered mace or nutmeg. Simmer steadily for five hours. When the water is too low, add that which is boiling. Put the meat on a platter, and the vegetables around it. Strain the liquor on to toasted bread in a soup-dish.

All these articles can be obtained at grocers or markets in our large cities, and of course can be procured in the country.

French Mutton Stew.—Take a leg of mutton and remove the large bone, leaving the bone at the small end as a handle; cut off also the bone below the knuckle, and fix it with skewers.

Put it in a stew-pan with a pinch of allspice, four onions, two cloves, two carrots, each cut in four pieces, a small bunch of parsley, two bay leaves, three sprigs of thyme, and *salt and pepper to the taste.* Add two ounces of bacon cut in slices, a quarter of a pint of broth, and cold water enough to cover it. After one hour of simmering, add a wine-glass of French brandy.

Let them simmer five hours longer, and then dish it; strain the sauce on it, and serve.

The American housekeeper by experiments can modify these foreign recipes to meet the taste of her family, and will find them *economical* modes of cooking, as well as healthful to most persons.

FRENCH MODES OF COOKING SOUPS AND STEWS.

The writer has examined the recipes of Gouffee, the chief French cook of the Queen of England, set forth in the expensive Royal Cook-Book; also those of Soyer and Professor Blot. She and her friends also have tested many of their recipes.

The following are most of the flavors used by them in cooking soups, stews, hashes, etc. Combination of these is recommended by those authors in these proportions:

One fourth of an ounce of thyme.
One fourth of an ounce of bay leaf.
One eighth of an ounce of marjoram.
One eighth of an ounce of rosemary.

Dry the above when fresh, mix in a mortar, and keep them corked tight in a glass bottle.

Also the following in these proportions:

Half an ounce of nutmeg.
Half an ounce of cloves.
One fourth of an ounce of black pepper.
One eighth of an ounce of Cayenne pepper.
Pound, mix, and keep corked tight in glass. In using these with salt, put one ounce of the last recipe to four ounces of salt. In making forcemeat and hashes, use at the rate of one ounce of this spiced salt to three pounds of meat.

Soup Powder,—Two ounces of parsley
Two ounces of winter savory.
Two ounces of sweet marjoram.
Two ounces of lemon-thyme.
One ounce of lemon-peel.
One ounce of sweet basil.
Dry, pound, sift, and keep in a tight-corked bottle.

Let the housekeeper add these flavors so that they will *not be strong*, but quite delicate, and then *make a rule for the cook.*
The peculiar excellence of French cooking is the combination of flavors, so that no one is predominant, and all are delicate in force and quantity.

IV.

SOUPS.

General Directions.

Most of the preceding stews will serve also fairly as soups, by adding more water. Rub salt into meat for soups, but not for stews, as the salt extracts the juices; and in stews the meat is to be eaten, while in soups properly so called it is only the liquor that is served. Put meat into cold water for soups, as *slowly* heating also extracts the juices. For this same reason, meat that is boiled for eating should be put into boiling water to keep the juices in it.

Always *skim often*, as soon as the water begins to simmer; and do not add the salt and other seasoning till the scum ceases to rise.

Do not boil after the juices are extracted, as too much boiling injures the flavor.

Never cool soup in metal, as there may be poison in the soldering or other parts.

If you flavor soup by vegetables, do not boil them in the soup, but in *very little* water, which is to be added to the soup with them, as it contains much of their flavor.

When onion is used for flavor, slice and fry it, and dredge on a little flour; add the water in which the vegetables for soup were boiled, or some meat broth, and then pour it into the soup. If you flavor with wine, soy, or catsup, put them into the tureen, and pour the soup upon them, as the flavor is lessened by putting them into the soup-kettle. Bread-crumbs, toast, or crackers also must be put in the tureen. Keep soup covered tight while boiling, to keep in flavors. If water is added, it must be boiling. The rule to guide in using salt and pepper is a heaping tea-spoonful of salt to a quart of water, and one sixth as much pepper. But as tastes are different, and the salt and pepper vary in strength, the housekeeper can, on trial, change the recipe with a pencil.

Soup stock is broth of any kind of meat prepared in large quantity, to keep on hand for gravies and soups. Beef and veal make the best stock. One hind shin of beef makes five quarts of stock, and one hind shin of veal makes three quarts. Wash and put into twice as much water as you wish to, to have soup, and simmer five or six hours.

All kinds of bones should be mashed and boiled five or six hours, to take out all the nutriment, the liquor then strained, and kept in earthenware or stone, not in tin. Take off the fat when cool.

Cool broth quickly, and it keeps longer.

Use a flat-bottom kettle, as less likely to scorch.

Soft water is best for soups; a little soda improves hard water.

Stock will keep three or four days in cool weather; not so long in warm. Keep it in a cool place. When used, heat to boiling point, and then take up and flavor.

Put in the salt and pepper when the meat is thoroughly done.

Meat soups are best the second day, if warmed slowly and taken up as soon as heated. If heated too long, they become insipid.

Thin soups must be strained. If to be made very clear, stir in one or two well-beaten eggs, with the shells, and let it boil half an hour.

Use the meat of the soup for a hash, warmed together with a little fat, and well seasoned.

Be *very* careful, in using bones and cold meats for soups, that none is *tainted*, for the soup may be ruined by a single bit of tainted meat or bone.

Potato Soup.—Take six large mealy potatoes, sliced and soaked an hour. Add one onion, sliced and tied in a rag, a quart of milk, and a quarter of a pound of salt pork cut in slices. Boil three quarters of an hour, and then add a table-spoonful of melted butter and a well-beaten egg, mixed in a cup of milk. This is a favorite soup with many, and easily made. Some omit the pork, and use salt and pepper to flavor it, and add one well-beaten *egg*.

Green Corn Soup.—This is very nice made with sweet corn put into seasoned soup stock.

Plain Beef Soup.—Put three pounds of beef and one chopped onion, tied in a rag, to three quarts of cold water. Simmer till the meat is very soft—say four hours; then add three tea-spoonfuls of salt, as much sugar, and half a tea-spoonful of pepper. Any other flavors may be added to suit the taste. Strain the soup, and save the meat for mince-meat or hash. Half a dozen sliced tomatoes will much improve this. Some would thicken with three or four tea-spoonfuls of potato-starch or flour.

Rich Beef Soup.—The following is a specimen of soups that are most stylish, rich, and demand most care in preparation:

Simmer six pounds of beef for six hours in six quarts of water, using the bones, broken in small pieces. Cool it, and take off the fat. Next day, an hour before dinner, take out the meat to use for hash or mincemeat, heat the liquor, throw in some salt to raise the scum, and skim it well. Then slice small, and boil in very little water, these vegetables: two turnips, two carrots, one head of celery, one quart of tomatoes, half a head of small white cabbage, one pint of green corn or Shaker corn, soaked over night. Cook the cabbage in two waters, throwing away the first. Boil the soup half an hour after these are put in. Season with salt, pepper, mace, and wine to suit the taste.

Green Pea Soup.—Boil the pods an hour in a gallon of water. Strain the liquor, and put into it four pounds of beef or mutton, and simmer one hour. Then add half the peas contained in half a peck of pods, and boil half an hour; then thicken with two great spoonfuls of flour, and season with salt and pepper. Three tomatoes, sliced, improve this.

Dried Bean Soup or Pea Soup.—Soak the beans, if dry, over night, and then boil till soft. Then strain them through a colander; and to each quart of liquor add a tea-spoonful of sugar, a tea-spoonful of salt, and a salt-spoonful of pepper. Add a beaten *egg*, a tea-cup of milk, and two spoonfuls of butter. A sliced onion improves it for some, and not for others; also, half the juice of a lemon when taken up. Canned sweet-corn, or common corn with sugar added, makes good *succotash* for winter.

Clam Soup.—Wash and boil the clams till they come out of their shells easily; then chop them, and put them back into the liquor, which should first be strained. Add a tea-cup of milk for each quart of soup; thicken with a little flour, into which has been worked as much butter as it will hold, and season with salt and pepper to suit the taste.

A Vegetable and Meat Soup for Summer.—Take three quarts of stock that is duly seasoned with sugar, salt, and pepper. Add two small onions, chopped fine, three small carrots, three small turnips, one stalk of celery, and a pint of green peas—all chopped fine. Let it simmer two hours, and then serve it.

Dried Pea Soup, with Salt Pork.—Soak a quart of split peas over night in soft water. Next morning wash them and put them in four quarts of water, with a tea-spoonful of sugar, two carrots, two small onions, and one stalk of celery—all cut in small pieces. Let them boil three hours. Boil a pound of salt pork in another pot for one hour; take off the skin, and put the pork in the soup, and then boil one hour longer.

Dried Bean or Pea Soup, with Meat Stock.—Soak a pint of beans or split peas over night in soft water. Then boil them in three quarts of soup-stock, duly seasoned with salt and pepper, with one small onion, one turnip, one stalk of celery, and six cloves—all cut in small pieces. Let it boil four or five hours. Strain through a colander.

Mutton Soup.—Boil four pounds of mutton in four quarts of water, with four heaping tea-spoonfuls of salt, one even tea-spoonful of pepper, two tea-spoonfuls of sugar, one small onion, two carrots, and two turnips—all cut fine—and one tea-cup of rice or broken macaroni. Boil the meat alone two hours; then add the rest, and boil one hour and a half longer.

French Vegetable Soup.—Take a leg of lamb, of moderate size, and four quarts of water. Of potatoes, carrots, cabbage, tomatoes, and turnips take a tea-cupful of each, chopped fine. Salt and black pepper at the rate of one heaping tea-spoonful of salt to each quart of water, and one sixth as much black pepper.

Wash the lamb, and put it into the four quarts of cold water. When the scum rises, take it off carefully with a skimmer. After having pared and chopped the vegetables, put them into the soup. Carrots require the most boiling, and should be put in first. This soup requires about three hours to boil.

Plain Calf's Head Soup.—Boil the head and feet in just water enough to cover them; when tender, take out the bones, cut in small pieces, and season with marjoram, thyme, cloves, salt, and pepper.

Put all into a pot, with the liquor, and four spoonfuls of butter; stew gently an hour; then, just as you take it up, add two or three glasses of port wine, and the yelks of three eggs boiled hard.

An Excellent Simple Mutton Soup.—Put a piece of the fore-quarter of mutton into salted water, enough to more than cover it, and simmer it slowly two hours. Then peel a dozen turnips, and six tomatoes, and quarter them, and boil them with the mutton till just tender enough to eat. Thicken the soup with pearl barley. Some use, instead of tomatoes, the juice and rind of a lemon. Use half a tea-cup of rice, if you have no pearl barley.

V.

HASHES.

These are the common ways of spoiling hashes: 1. By frying, instead of merely heating them. Melted butter and oils are good and healthful when only heated, but are unhealthful when fried. 2. Dredging in flour, which, not being well cooked, imparts a raw taste of dough. 3. Using too much water, making them vapid; or too much fat or gravy, making them gross. 4. Using too much or too little salt and other seasoning. The following recipes will save from these mistakes, if exactly followed. When water is recommended in these recipes, *cold gravy* will be better, in which case, the *butter* may be omitted:

A Seasoned Hash of any Fresh Meats.—Chop, but not very fine, any kinds of fresh meat, but be sure not to put in any that is tainted. To a common tumblerful of chopped meat put three table-spoonfuls of water, a tea-spoonful of sugar, a heaping tea-spoonful of salt, a salt-spoonful of pepper, and butter the size of half an egg. Warm, but do not fry: and when hot, break in three eggs, and stir till they are hardened a little; then serve. Bread-crumbs may be added. This may be put on buttered toast or served alone. This and all the following hashes may be varied in flavor, by adding, in delicate proportions, the mixed flavors on another page.

A Hash of Cold Fresh Meats and Potatoes.—Take two tumblerfuls of meat of any kind, chopped. Add as much cold potatoes, also chopped, two table-spoonfuls of sweet butter in six table-spoonfuls of hot water, and two tea-spoonfuls of salt. Sprinkle half a tea spoonful of pepper over the meat, and also a spoonful of sugar; mix all, and warm about twenty minutes, but not so as to boil or fry. Tomatoes improve this.

Meat Hash with Eggs, (very nice.)—To a tumblerful of fresh cold meat cut in pieces about the size of peas, put three table-spoonfuls of hot water, two spoonfuls of butter, a tea-spoonful of sugar, two tea-spoonfuls of salt, and a salt-spoonful of pepper. Mix all, warm but not fry; and when hot, break in four eggs, and stir till they are hardened. Spread on buttered toast or serve alone. When eggs are used, the meat should not be chopped fine.

A Meat Hash with Tomatoes.—Cut up a pint of tomatoes into a saucepan, and when boiling hot, add the cold meat in thin slices, with a table-spoonful of sugar, and salt and pepper, at the rate of a tea-spoonful of salt and half a tea-spoonful of pepper to each tumblerful of meat.

A Nice Beef Hash.—Make a gravy of melted butter, or take cold gravy; season with salt, pepper, and currant jelly or vinegar. Cut cold roast beef or the remnants of cold stake into mouthfuls, and put into the gravy till heated, but not to fry.

Or, season this gravy with the crushed juice of fresh tomatoes or tomato catsup.

A Simple and Excellent Veal Hash.—Chop cold veal very fine; butter pudding-dish, and make alternate layers of veal and powdered crackers till the dish is full, the first layer of meat being at the bottom. Then beat up two eggs, and add a pint or less of milk, seasoned well with salt and pepper, and two or three spoonfuls of melted butter. Pour this over the meat and crackers; cover with a plate, and bake about half an hour. Remove the plate awhile, and let the top brown a little. This is the best way to cook veal, and children are very fond of it.

Rice and Cold Meats.—Chop remnants of fresh meats with salt pork or cold ham. Season with salt and pepper and a little sugar; add two eggs and a little butter. Then make alternate layers with this and slices of cold boiled rice, and bake it half an hour.

Bread-Crumbs and Cold Meats.—Take any remnants of cooked fresh meats, and chop them fine with bits of ham or salt pork. Season with salt and pepper; add three eggs and a little milk, and then thicken with pounded bread-crumbs. Bake it as a pudding, or warm it for a hash, or cook it in flat cakes on a griddle.

A Meat Hash with Bread-Crumbs,—One tea-spoonful of flour, (or potato or corn-starch,) wet in four tea-spoonfuls of cold water. Stir it into a tea-cupful of boiling water, and put in a salt-spoonful of pepper, two tea-spoonfuls of salt, a tea-spoonful of sugar, and two table-spoonfuls of sweet butter. Use cold gravy instead of butter, if you have it. Set this in a stew-pan where it will be kept hot, but not fry. Chop the meat very fine, and mix with it while chopping half as much dried bread-crumbs. Put this into the gravy, and let it heat only ten minutes, and then serve it on buttered toast. Tomatoes, one or two, improve this.

A Hash of Cold Beefsteak alone or with Potatoes and Turnips.— Make a paste with a heaping tea-spoonful of flour in two tea-spoonfuls of water. Stir it into a, tea-cup and a half of boiling water, with a salt-spoonful of black pepper, a half tea-spoonful of sugar, and two tea-spoonfuls of salt. Let it stand where it will be hot but not boil. Cut the beef into mouthfuls, and also as much cold boiled potatoes and half as much boiled turnips. Mix all, and then add two table-spoonfuls of butter, (or some cold gravy,) and a table-spoonful of tomato catsup, or two sliced tomatoes. Warm, but do not fry, for ten minutes.

When beef gravy is used, take less salt and pepper.

This is a good recipe for cold beef without vegetables.

A Hash of Cold Mutton (or Venison) and Vegetables.—Prepare as in the preceding recipe, but add one onion sliced fine, to hide the strong mutton taste. If onion is left out, put in a wine-glass of grape or currant jelly. If the vegetables are left out, put in a little less pepper and salt.

A Hash of Corned Beef.—Chop the meat very fine, fat and lean together; add twice as much cold potatoes chopped fine. For each tumblerful of this add butter half the size of a hen's egg melted in half a tea-cup of hot water, a salt-spoonful of pepper and another of salt. Heat very hot, but do not let it fry. Some would add parsley or other sweet herb.

A Hash of Cold Ham.—Chop, not very fine, fat and lean together. Add twice the quantity of bread-crumbs chopped but not fine. Heat it hot, then break in two eggs for every tumblerful of the hash. A tea-spoonful of sugar improves it, and a salt-spoonful of pepper.

Meats warmed over.—Veal is best made into hashes. If it is liked more simply cooked, chop it fine, put in water just enough to moisten it, butter, salt, pepper, and a little juice of a lemon. Some like a little lemon-rind grated in. Heat it through, but do not let it fry. Put it on buttered toast, and garnish it with slices of lemon.

Cold salted or fresh beef is good chopped fine with pepper, salt, and catsup, and water enough to moisten a little. Add some butter just before taking it up, and do not let it fry, only heat it hot. It injures cooked meat to cook it again. Cold fowls make a nice dish to have them cut up in mouthfuls; add some of the gravy and giblet sauce, a little butter and pepper, and then heat them through.

A nice Way of Cooking Cold Meats.—Chop the meat fine, add salt, pepper, a little onion, or else tomato catsup; fill a tin bread-pan one third full, cover it over with boiled potatoes salted and mashed with cream or milk, lay bits of butter on the top and set it into a Dutch or stove oven for fifteen or twenty minutes.

A Hash of Cold Meat for Dinner, (very good.)—Peel six large tomatoes and one onion, and slice them. Add a spoonful of sugar, salt and pepper, and a bit of butter the size of a hen's egg, and half a pint of cold water. Shave up the meat into small bits, as thin as thick pasteboard. Dredge flour over it, say two tea-spoonfuls, or a little less. Simmer the meat with all the rest for *half an hour*, and then serve it, and it is very fine.

Dried tomatoes can be used. When you have no tomatoes, make a gravy with water, pepper, salt, and butter, or cold gravy; slice an onion in it, add tomato catsup, (two or three spoonfuls,) and then prepare the meat as above, and simmer it in this gravy *half an hour*.

Souse.—Cleanse pigs' ears and feet and soak them a week in salt and water, changing the water every other day. Boil eight or ten hours till tender. When cold, put on salt, and pour on hot spiced vinegar. Warm them in lard or butter.

Tripe.—Scrape and scour it thoroughly, soak it in salt and water a week, changing it every other day. Boil it eight or ten hours, till tender; then pour on spiced hot vinegar and broil it.

VI.

BOILED MEATS.

An Excellent Way to cook Tough Beef.—To eight pounds of beef put four quarts of water, two table-spoonfuls of salt, half a tea-spoonful of pepper, three tea-spoonfuls of vinegar, and four tea-spoonfuls of sugar. Put it on at eight in the morning, and let it simmer slowly till the water is more than half gone; then skim off the grease, and set it in the stove-oven till the water is all gone but about a tea-cupful, which is for gravy, and may be thickened a little. Add *boiling* water, if it goes too fast, (for in some kinds of weather it will evaporate much faster than in other days.) This dish should be *very* tender, and is excellent cold, especially if it is pressed under a heavy weight. This was a favorite soldier's dish; and tough meat is as good as it is tender, when thus cooked.

Boiled Ham.—The best way to cook a ham is first to wash it; then take off the skin and bake it in a pan, with a little water in it, in a stove or brick oven, till tender, which is found by a fork piercing easily. Allow twenty minutes for each pound.

To boil a ham, soak it over night; then wash in two waters, using a brush. Boil slowly, and allow fifteen minutes for each pound. When cold, take off the skin, and ornament with dots of pepper and fringed paper tied around the shank.

A nice way to treat a cold boiled ham is, after removing the skin, to rub it over with beaten egg, and then spread over powdered cracker, wet with milk, and let it brown in the oven. Boiled ham is much improved by setting it in the oven half an hour, making it sweeter, while the fat that tries out is useful for cooking.

Boiled Beef.—Put it in salted water, (a tea-spoonful for each quart;) have enough to cover it. Skim well just before it begins to boil, and as long as the scum rises. Allow about fifteen minutes to each pound, or more for beef. Drain well, and serve with vegetables boiled separately.

Boiled Fowls.—Wash the inside carefully with soda water, to remove any taint. Stuff with seasoned bread-crumbs, or cracker, wet up with eggs, and sew up the openings. Put them in *boiling* water, enough to cover, and let them simmer gently till tender. It is a good plan to wrap in a cloth dredged with flour.

Fricasseed Fowls.—Cut them up, and put in a pot, with cold water enough to cover. Put some salt pork over, and let them simmer slowly till very tender and the water mostly gone. When done, stir in a cup of milk, mixed with two well-beaten eggs, first mixing slowly some of the hot liquor with the milk and eggs.

Some fry the pork first, thus increasing the flavor, and others leave it out.

To Boil a Leg or Shoulder of Veal, or Mutton, or Lamb.—Mutton should be cooked more rare than any other meat. Make a stuffing of chopped bread, seasoned with pepper and salt, and mixed with one or two eggs. Make deep gashes in the meat, (or, better, take out the bone;) fill the openings with stuffing, and sew them up. Wrap it tight in a cloth, and put it so as to be covered with water, salted at the rate of a tea-spoonful to each quart. Let it simmer slowly about two or three hours. Skim thoroughly just before it comes to boiling heat. If needful, add *boiling* water. Save the water for broth for next day. If you pour cold water on the cloth before removing it, and let it stand two minutes, it improves the looks.

Calf' Feet.—Wash and scrape till very clean. Boil three hours in four quarts of water salted with four even tea-spoonfuls of salt. Take out the bones, and put the rest into a sauce-pan, with three table-spoonfuls of butter, two table-spoonfuls of vinegar, a great-spoonful of sugar, and a salt-spoonful of pepper. Add three tea-cups of the liquor in which the feet were boiled; dredge in some flour, and simmer for fifteen minutes. Garnish with sliced lemon. (Save the liquor to make calf's foot jelly.)

Calf's Liver and Sweetbreads.—These are best split open, boiled, and then dressed with pepper, salt, and butter.

To cook Kidneys.— Wash them clean, and split them. Heat them half an hour in a sauce-pan, without water. Then wash them again, and cover them with a pint of water, having in it a tea-spoonful of salt and a salt-spoonful of pepper. Boil one hour, and then take off the skin. Cut them in mouthfuls; add two great-spoonfuls of butter, more salt and hot water, if needed, and let them simmer fifteen minutes.

Pillau, a Favorite Dish in the South.—Fricassee a chicken with slices of salt pork, or with sweet butter or sweet cream. Put the chicken, when cooked, in a bake-dish, and cover it with boiled rice, seasoned with salt, pepper, and one dozen allspice. Pile the rice, pour on some melted butter, smooth it, and cover with yelk of an egg. Bake half an hour.

To Boil Smoked Tongues.—Soak in cold water only two hours, as long soaking lessens sweetness. Wash them, and boil four or five hours, according to the size. When done, take off the skin and garnish with parsley. A table-spoonful of sugar for each tongue, put in the water, improves them.

To boil Corned Beef.—Do not soak it, but wash it, and put it in *hot* water, to keep in the juices; allow a pint for each pound. Skim just before it begins to boil. Let it simmer slowly, and allow twenty-five minutes for every pound. Keep it covered with water, adding boiling hot water, if needed. It is much improved for eating cold by pressing it with a board and heavy stone. It is an excellent piece of economy to save the water to use for soup.

Some think it an improvement to put on a little sugar, and pour a little vinegar on before boiling. Some like to boil turnips, potatoes, and cabbage with it. In that case, they must be peeled, and the potatoes soaked two hours.

To boil Partridges or Pigeons.—Cleanse and rinse the insides with soda-water, and then with pure water. Wrap them in a damp floured cloth; put them into boiling water which is salted at the rate of a heaping tea-spoonful to a quart; also, two tea-spoonfuls of sugar and a salt-spoonful of pepper. Simmer them twenty minutes to half an hour. When done, make a sauce of butter rubbed into flour and half a cup of milk; put the birds into a dish and pour on this sauce. Some would add cut parsley, or other flavors.

To boil Ducks.—Let them lie in hot water two hours. Then wrap in a cloth dredged with flour; put them in cold water, salted at the rate of a half a tea-spoonful for each pint. Add a tea-spoonful of sugar for each pint. Let them simmer half an hour; then take them up, and pour over them a sauce made of melted butter rubbed into flour, and seasoned with lemon-juice, salt, and pepper, and thinned with gravy or hot water.

Wild ducks must be soaked in salt and water the night previous, to remove the fishy taste, and then in the morning put in fresh water, which should be changed once or twice.

To boil a Turkey.—Make a stuffing for the craw of chopped bread and butter, cream, oysters, and the yelks of eggs. Sew it in, and dredge flour over the turkey, and put it in hot water to boil, with a spoonful of salt in it, and enough water to cover it well. Let it simmer for two hours and a half, or, if small, less time. Skim it while boiling. It will look nicer if wrapped in a cloth dredged with flour while cooking.

Serve it with drawn butter, in which are put some oysters.

VII.

ROAST AND BAKED MEATS.

The beef of an ox is best, and the next best is that of a heifer. The best pieces for roasting are the second cut of the sirloin, the second cut of the ribs, and the back part of the rump.

The art of roasting well consists of turning the meat often, to prevent burning, and basting often, to make it juicy.

Never dredge flour into gravies, as it makes lumps. Strain all gravies.

Brown Flour for Meat Gravies.—This is used to thicken meat gravies, to give a good color. It is prepared by putting flour on a tin plate in a hot oven, stirring it often until well browned; it must be kept, corked, in a jar, and shaken occasionally.

Roast Beef.—A piece of beef weighing ten pounds requires about two hours to roast in a tin oven before a fire. Allow ten minutes for each pound over or under this weight. Have the spit and oven clean and bright. They should have been washed before they grew cold from the last roasting.

Put the meat on the spit so that it will be evenly balanced; set the bony side toward the fire; let it roast slowly at first, turning it often; and when all sides are partly cooked, move it nearer the fire. If allowed to scorch at first, it will not cook in the middle without burning the outside.

Baste often with the drippings and with salted water, (about half a pint of water with half a tea-spoonful of salt,) which has been put in the oven bottom. Just before taking up, dredge on some flour, mixed with a little salt; then baste and set it near the fire, turning it so as to brown it all over alike. Half an hour before it is done, pour off the gravy, season it with salt and pepper, and thicken with corn or potato-starch, or flour.

To roast in a Cook Stove.—Put the meat in an iron pan, with three or four gills of water, and a tea-spoonful of salt. Turn it occasionally, that it may cook evenly, and baste often. When done, dredge on some salted flour, baste again, and set it back till browned.

Roast Pork.—Cover a spare-rib with greased paper, till half done; then dredge with flour, and baste with the gravy. Just before taking it up, cover the surface with cracker or bread-crumbs, wet up with pepper, salt, and powdered sage; let it cook ten minutes longer, and then baste again. Skim the gravy, thicken it with brown flour, season with a little powdered sage and lemon-juice, or vinegar; strain it, and pour over the meat. Pork must be cooked slowly and very thoroughly, and served with apple sauce. Tomato catsup improves the gravy.

Roast Mutton.—The leg of mutton may be boiled. The shoulder and loin should always be roasted.

Put the meat in the oven or roaster, and then pour boiling hot water over it, to keep in the juices. Baste often with salt and water at first and then with the gravy. With a hot fire, allow ten minutes for each pound. If there is danger of burning, cover the outside with oiled white paper. Skim the gravy; strain it and thicken with brown flour. Serve with acid jelly. Lamb requires less time in roasting; but mutton should be rare. Make a brown gravy, and serve with currant jelly.

Roast Veal.—Follow the above directions for roasting mutton, except to allow more time, as veal should be cooked more than mutton. Allow twenty minutes to each pound, and baste often. Too much roasting and little basting spoil veal. To be served with apple-sauce. It much improves roast veal to cut slits in it, and insert bits of salt pork.

Roast Poultry.—No fowl should be bought when the entrails are not drawn; and the insides should always be washed with soda-water—a tea-spoonful of soda to a pint of water. Rinse out with fair water. Stuff with seasoned bread-crumbs, wet up with eggs. Sew and tie the stuffing in thoroughly. Allow about ten minutes' cooking for each pound, more or less, according to the fire and size of the fowl.

Put a grate in the bake-pan, with a tea-cup of salted water. Dredge the fowl with flour at first, and baste often. Strain the gravy, and add the giblets, chopped fine. Many dislike the liver, and so leave it out. If fowls are bought with the intestines in, or if they have been kept too long, the use of soda-water, and then rinsing with pure water, will often prevent the tainted taste; so it is well to do this, except when it is certain that the fowl is just killed. Put a tea-spoonful of soda to a pint of water.

Pot-Pie, of Beef, Veal, or Chicken.—The best way to make the crust is as follows: Peel, boil, and mash a dozen potatoes; add a tea-spoonful of salt, two table-spoonfuls of butter, and half a cup of milk, or cream. Then stiffen it with flour, till you can roll it. Be sure to get all the lumps out of the potatoes. Some persons leave out the butter.

Some roll butter into the dough of bread; others make a raised biscuit, with but little shortening; others make a plain soda pie-crust. But none are so good and healthful as the potato-crust; so choose what is best for all.

To prepare the meat, first fry half a dozen slices of salt pork, and then cut up the meat and pork, and boil them in just water enough to cover them, till the meat is nearly cooked. Then peel a dozen potatoes, and slice them thin. Roll the crust half an inch thick, and cut it into oblong pieces. Then put alternate layers of crust, potatoes, and meat, till all is used. The top and bottom layer must be crust. Divide the pork so as to have some in each layer.

Lastly, pour on the liquor in which the meat was boiled, until it just covers the whole, and let it simmer till the top crust is well cooked—say half or three quarters of an hour. Season the liquor with salt, at the rate of a tea-spoonful for each quart, and one sixth as much pepper. If you have occasion to add more liquor, or water, it must be *boiling hot,* or the crust will be spoilt.

The excellence of this pie depends on having light crust, and therefore the meat must first be *nearly cooked* before putting it in the pie; and the crust must be in only just long enough to cook, or it will be clammy and hard.

Mutton and Beef-Pie.—Line a dish with a crust made of potatoes, as directed in the Chicken Pot-Pie. Broil the meat ten minutes, after pounding it till the fibres are broken. Cut the meat thin, and put it in layers, with thin slices of broiled salt pork; season with butter, the size of a hen's egg, salt, pepper, (and either wine or catsup, if liked;) put in water till it nearly covers the meat, and dredge in considerable flour; cover it with the paste, and bake it an hour and half, if quite thick. Cold meats are good cooked over in this way. Cut a slit in the centre of the cover.

Chicken-Pie.—Joint and boil two chickens in salted water, just enough to cover them, and simmer slowly for half an hour. Line a dish with potato crust, as directed in the recipe for pot-pie; then, when cold, put the chicken in layers, with thin slices of broiled pork, butter, the size of a goose egg, cut in small pieces. Put in enough of liquor, in which the meat was boiled, to reach the surface; salt and pepper each layer; dredge in a little flour, and cover all with a light, thick crust. Ornament the top with the crust, and bake about one hour in a hot oven. Make a small slit in the centre of the crust. If it begins to scorch, lay a paper over a short time.

Rice Chicken-Pie.—Line a pudding-dish with slices of broiled ham; cut up a boiled chicken, and nearly fill the dish, filling in with gravy or melted butter; add minced onions, if you like, or a little curry powder.

Then pile boiled rice to fill all interstices, and cover the top quite thick. Bake it for half or three quarters of an hour.

Potato-Pie.—Take mashed potatoes, seasoned with salt, butter, and milk, and line a baking-dish. Lay upon it slices of cold meats of any kind, with salt, pepper, catsup, and butter or gravy. Put on another layer of potatoes, and then another of cold meat, as before. Lastly, on the top put a cover of potatoes.

Bake it till it is thoroughly warmed through, and serve it in the dish in which it is baked, setting it in or upon another.

Calf's Head.—Take out the brains and boil the head, feet, and lights in salted water, just enough to cover them, about two hours. When they have boiled nearly an hour and a half, tie the brains in a cloth and put them in to boil with the rest. They should be skinned, and soaked half an hour in cold water. When the two hours have expired, take up the whole, mash the brains fine, and season them with bread-crumbs, pepper, salt, and a glass of port or claret, and use them for sauce. Let the liquor remain for a soup the next day. It serves more handsomely to remove all the bones. Serve with a gravy of drawn butter.

VIII.

BROILED AND FRIED MEATS AND RELISHES.

Broiled Mutton or Lamb Chops.—Cut off and the skinny part, which only turns black and can not be eaten. Put a little pepper and salt on each one, and broil by a quick fire. Mutton chops should be rare.

Broiled Beefsteak.—Have the steak cut three quarters of an inch to an inch in thickness. The sirloin and porter-house are the best. The art of cooking steak will depend on a good fire and turning often after it begins to drip. When done, lay it on a hot platter, season with butter, pepper, and salt; cover with another hot platter, and send to the table. Use beef-tongs, as pricking lets out the juices. *Slow* cooking and *much* cooking spoils a seak.

Broiled Fresh Pork.—Cut in thin slices, broil quickly and very thoroughly; then season with salt, pepper, and powdered sage.

Broiled Ham.—Cut in *thin* slices, and soak fifteen minutes in hot water. Pour off this and soak again as long. Wipe dry and broil over a quick fire, and then pepper it. Ham that is already cooked rare is best for broiling.

Broiled Sweetbreads.—The best way to cook sweetbreads is to broil them thus: Parboil them, and then put them on a clean gridiron for broiling. When delicately browned, take them off and roll in melted butter on a plate to prevent their being dry and hard. Some cook them on griddle well buttered, turning frequently; and some put narrow strips of fat salt pork on them while cooking.

Broiled Veal.—Cut it thin, and put thin slices of salt pork on the top after it is laid on the gridiron, and broil both together. When turning, put the pork again on the top. When the veal is thoroughly cooked, brown the pork a little by itself, while the veal stands on a hot dish.

A good Pork Relish.—Broil thin slices of fresh pork, first pouring on boiling water to lessen saltness. Cut them in small mouthfuls, and add butter, pepper, and salt.

FRIED MEATS AND RELISHES.

The most slovenly and unhealthful mode of cooking is frying, as it usually is done. If the fat is very hot, and the articles are put in and taken out exactly at the right time, it is well enough. But fried fat is hard to digest, and most fried food is soaked with it, so that only a strong stomach can digest it. Almost every thing that is fried might be better cooked on a griddle slightly oiled. A griddle should always be oiled only just enough to keep from sticking. It is best to fry in lard not salted, and this is better than butter. Mutton and beef suet are good for frying. When the lard seems hot, try it by throwing in a bit of bread. When taking up fried articles, drain off the fat on a wire sieve.

A nice Way of Cooking Calf's or Pig's Liver.—Cut in slices half an inch thick, pour on boiling water, and then pour it off *entirely;* then let the liver brown in its own juices, turning it till it looks brown on both sides. Take it up, and pour into the frying-pan enough cold water to make as much gravy as you wish; then sliver in a *very* little onion; add a little salt and nutmeg, and a bit of butter to season it; let it boil up once, then put back the liver for a minute longer.

Beef Liver.—Cut it in slices half an inch thick, pour boiling water on it, broil it with thin slices of pork dipped in flour, cut it in mouthfuls, and heat it with butter, pepper, and salt for three or four minutes.

Egg Omelet.—Beat the yolks of six eggs, and add a cup of milk, half a tea-spoonful of salt, and a pinch of pepper. Pour into hot fat, and cook till just stiffened. Turn it on to a platter brown side uppermost. Some add minced cooked ham, or cold meat chopped and salted. Others put in chopped cauliflower or asparagus cooked and cold.

Frizzled Beef.—Sliver smoked beef, pour on boiling water to freshen it, then pour off the water, and frizzle the beef in butter.

Veal Cheese.—Prepare equal quantities of sliced boiled veal and boiled smoked tongue, or ham sliced. Pound each separately in a mortar, moistening with butter as you proceed. Then take a stone jar, or tin can, and mix them in it, so that it will, when cut, look mottled and variegated. Press it hard, and pour on melted butter. Keep it covered in a dry place. To be used at tea in slices.

A Codfish Relish.—Take thin slivers of codfish, lay them on hot coals, and when done to a yellowish brown, set them on the table.

Another Way.—Sliver the codfish fine, pour on boiling water, drain it off, and add butter and a very little pepper, and heat them three or four minutes, but do not let them fry.

Salt Herrings.—Heat them on a gridiron, remove the skin, and then set them, on the table.

IX.

PICKLES.

Do not keep pickles in common earthenware, as the glazing contains lead, and combines with the vinegar.

Vinegar for pickling should be sharp, but not the sharpest kind, as it injures the pickles. Wine or cider vinegar is reliable. Much manufactured vinegar is sold that ruins pickles and is unhealthful. If you use copper, bell-metal, or brass vessels for pickling, never allow the vinegar to cool in them, as it then is poisonous. Add a table-spoonful of alum and a tea-cup of salt to each three gallons of vinegar, and tie up a bag with pepper, ginger-root, and spices of all sorts in it, and you have vinegar prepared for any kind of common pickling, and in many cases all that is needed is to throw the fruit in and keep it in till wanted.

Keep pickles only in wood, or stone-ware.

Any thing that has held grease will spoil pickles.

Stir pickles occasionally, and if there are soft ones, take them out, scald the vinegar, and pour it hot over the pickles. Keep enough vinegar to cover them well. If it is weak, take fresh vinegar, and pour on hot. Do not boil vinegar or spice over five minutes.

Sweet Pickles, (a great favorite.)—One pound of sugar, one quart of vinegar, two pounds of fruit. Boil fifteen minutes, skim well, put in the fruit and let it boil till half cooked. For peaches, flavor with cinnamon and mace; for plums and all dark fruit, use allspice and cloves.

To pickle Tomatoes.—As you gather them, leave an inch or more of stem; throw them into cold vinegar. When you have enough, take them out, and scald some spices, tied in a bag, in good vinegar; add a little sugar, and pour it hot over them.

To pickle Peaches.—Take ripe but hard peaches, wipe off the down, stick a few cloves into them, and lay them in *cold* spiced vinegar. In three months, they will be sufficiently pickled, and also retain much of their natural flavor.

To pickle Peppers.—Take green peppers, take the seeds out carefully so as not to mangle them, soak them nine days in salt and water, changing it every day, and keep them in a warm place. Stuff them with chopped cabbage, seasoned with cloves, cinnamon, and mace; put them in cold spiced vinegar.

To pickle Nasturtions.—Soak them three days in salt and water as you collect them, changing it once in three days; and when you have enough, pour off the brine, and pour on scalding hot vinegar.

To pickle Onions.—Peel, and boil in milk and water ten minutes, drain off the milk and water, and pour scalding spiced vinegar on to them.

To pickle Gherkins.—Keep them in strong brine till they are yellow, them take them out and turn on hot spiced vinegar, and keep them in it, in a warm place, till they turn green. Then turn off the vinegar, and add a fresh supply of hot, spiced vinegar.

To pickle Mushrooms.—Stew them in salted water, just enough to keep them from sticking. When tender, pour off the water, and pour on hot spiced vinegar. Then cork them tight, if you wish to keep them long. Poison ones will turn black if an onion is stewed with them, and then all must be thrown away.

To pickle Cucumbers.—Wash the cucumbers in cold water, being careful not to bruise or break them. Make a brine of rock or blown salt (rock is the best,) strong enough to bear up an egg or potato, and of sufficient quantity to cover the cucumbers.

Put them into an oaken tub, or stone-ware jar, and pour the brine over them. In twenty-four hours, they should be stirred up from the bottom with the hand. The third day pour off the brine, scald it, and pour it over the cucumbers. Let them stand in the brine nine days, scalding it every third day, as described above. Then take the cucumbers into a tub, rinse them in cold water, and if they are too salt, let them stand in it a few hours. Drain them from the water, put them back into the tub or jar, which must be washed clean from the brine. Scald vinegar sufficient to cover them, and pour it upon them. Cover them tight, and in a week they will be ready for use. If spice is wanted, it may be tied in a linen cloth and put into the jar with the pickles, or scalded with the vinegar, and the bag thrown into the pickle-jar. If a white scum rises, take it off and scald the vinegar, and pour it back. A small lump of alum added to the vinegar improves the hardness of the cucumbers.

Pickled Walnuts.—Take a hundred nuts, an ounce of cloves, an ounce of allspice, an ounce of nutmeg, an ounce of whole pepper, an ounce of race ginger, an ounce of horse-radish, half pint of mustard-seed, and four cloves of garlic, tied in a bag.

Wipe the nuts, prick with a pin, and put them in a pot, sprinkling the spice as you lay them in; then add two table-spoonfuls of salt; boil sufficient vinegar to fill the pot, and pour it over the nuts and spice. Cover the jar close, and keep it for a year, when the pickles will be ready for use.

Butternuts may be made in the same manner, if they are taken when green, and soft enough to be stuck through with the head of a pin. Put them for a week or two in weak brine, changing it occasionally. Before putting in the brine, rub them about with broom in brine, to cleanse the skins. Then proceed as for the walnuts.

The vinegar makes an excellent catsup.

Mangoes.—Take the latest growth of young muskmelons, cut out a small piece from one side and empty them. Scrape the outside smooth, and soak them four days in strong salt and water. If you wish to green them, put vine leaves over and under, with bits of alum, and steam them awhile. Then powder cloves, pepper, and nutmeg in equal portions, and sprinkle on the inside, and fill them with strips of horse-radish, small bits of calamus, bits of cinnamon and mace, a clove or two, a very small onion, nasturtions, and then American mustard seed to fill the crevices. Put back the piece cut out, and sew it on, and then sew the mango in cotton cloth. Lay all in a stone jar, the cut side upward.

Boil sharp vinegar a few minutes with half a tea-cup of salt, and a table-spoonful of alum to three gallons of vinegar, and turn it on to the melons.

Keep dried barberries for garnishes, and when you use them, turn a little of the above vinegar of the mangoes heated boiling hot on to them, and let them swell a few hours. Sliced and salted cabbage with this vinegar poured on hot is very good.

Fine pickled Cabbage.—Shred red and white cabbage, spread it in layers in a stone jar, with salt over each layer. Put two spoonfuls of whole black pepper, and the same quantity of allspice, cloves, and cinnamon, in a bag, and scald them in two quarts of vinegar, and pour the vinegar over the cabbage, and cover it tight. Use it in two days after.

An excellent Way of preparing Tomatoes to eat with Meat.—Peel and slice ripe tomatoes, sprinkling on a little salt as you proceed. Drain off the juice, and pour on hot spiced vinegar.

To pickle Martinoes.—Gather them when you can run a pin-head into them, and after wiping them, keep them ten days in weak brine, changing it every other day. Then wipe them, and pour over boiling spiced vinegar. In four weeks, they will be ready for use. It is a fine pickle.

A convenient Way to pickle Cucumbers.—Put some spiced vinegar in a jar, with little salt in it. Every time you gather a mess, pour boiling vinegar on them, with a little alum in it. Then put them in the spiced vinegar. Keep the same vinegar for scalding all. When you have enough, take all from the spiced vinegar, and scald in the alum vinegar two or three minutes, till green, and then put them back in the spiced vinegar.

Indiana Pickles.—Take green tomatoes, and slice them. Put them in a basket to drain in layers, with salt scattered over them, say a tea-cupful to each gallon. Next day, slice one quarter the quantity of onions, and lay the onions and tomatoes in alternate layers in a jar, with spice intervening. Then fill the jar with cold vinegar. Tomatoes picked as they ripen, and just thrown into cold spiced vinegar, are a fine pickle, and made with very little trouble.

To pickle Cauliflower, or Broccoli.—Keep them twenty-four hours in strong brine, and then take them out and heat the brine, and pour it on scalding hot, and let them stand till next day Drain them, and throw them into spiced vinegar.

X.

SAUCES AND SALADS.

SUCCESS in preparing savory meats and salads depends greatly on the different sauces, and these demand extra care in preparation and in flavoring. The following is a sauce that is a great favorite, and serves for some meats, for fish, for macaroni, and for some salads:

Milk and Egg Sauce, (excellent.)—Take eight table-spoonfuls of butter and mix it with a table-spoonful of flour, add a pint of milk and heat it, stirring constantly till it thickens a little. Then beat the yelk of an egg in a table-spoonful of water and mix it well with the sauce, taking care that it does not boil, but only be very hot. For fish, add to the above a table-spoonful of vinegar or lemon-juice and a little of the peel grated. Some add parsley chopped; and for boiled fowls, add chopped oysters. Fine bread-crumbs are better than flour for thickening. For macaroni, make in the dish alternate layers with that and grated cheese, and then pour on this sauce before baking, and it is very fine. Some omit the cheese

Drawn Butter.—Take six table-spoonfuls of butter, half a tea-spoonful of salt, two tea-spoonfuls of flour or of fine bread-crumbs worked into the butter, and one tea-cup of hot water. Heat very hot, but do not let it boil. Two hard-boiled and chopped eggs improve it much. For fish, add a table-spoonful of vinegar and chopped capers or green nasturtion seeds.

Mint Sauce for Roast Lamb.—Chop three table-spoonfuls of green mint, and add a heaping table-spoonful of sugar and half a coffee-cup of vinegar. Stir them while heating, and cool before using.

Cranberry Sauce.—Wash well and put a tea-cup of water to every quart of cranberries. Let them stew about an hour and a half, then take up and sweeten abundantly. Some strain them through a colander, then sweeten largely and then put into moulds. To be eaten with fowls.

Apple Sauce.—Core and slice the best apples you can get, cook till soft, then add sugar and a little butter. Serve it with fresh pork and veal.

Walnut or Butternut Catsup.—Gather the nuts when they can be pierced with a pin. Beat them to a soft pulp and let them lie for two weeks in quite salt water, say a small handful of salt to every twenty, and water enough to cover them. Drain off this liquor, and pour on a pint of boiling vinegar and mix with the nuts, and then strain it out. To each quart of this liquor put three table-spoonfuls of pepper, one of ginger, two spoonfuls of powdered cloves, and three spoonfuls of grated nutmeg. Boil an hour and bottle when cold. See that the spice is equally mixed. Do not use mushroom catsup, as the above is as good and not so dangerous.

Mock Capers.—Dry the green but full-grown nasturtion seeds for a day in the sun, then put them in jars and pour on spiced vinegar. These are good for fish sauce, in drawn butter.

Salad Dressing.—Mash fine two boiled potatoes, and add a tea-spoonful of mustard, two of salt, four of sweet-oil, three of sharp vinegar, and the yelks of two well-boiled eggs rubbed fine. Mix first the egg and potatoes, add the mustard and salt, and gradually mix in the oil, stirring vigorously the while. Stir in the vinegar last. Melted butter may be used in place of sweet-oil. The more a salad dressing is stirred, the better it will be.

Turkey or Chicken Salad, also a Lettuce Salad.—Take one quarter chopped meat (the white meat of the fowl is the best for this purpose) and three quarters chopped celery, well mixed, and pour over it a sauce containing the yelks of two hard-boiled eggs chopped, a tea-spoonful of salt, half a salt-spoonful of black pepper, half a tea-spoonful of mustard, three tea-spoonfuls of sugar, half a tea-cupful of vinegar, and three tea-spoonfuls of sweet-oil or of melted butter. Mix the salt, pepper, sugar, and mustard thoroughly, whip a raw egg and add slowly, stir in the sweet-oil or melted butter, mixing it well and very slowly, and lastly add the vinegar. Garnish with rings of whites of eggs boiled hard. Chopped pickles may be added and white cabbage in place of the celery.

Tomato Catsup.—Boil a peck of tomatoes, strain through a colander, and then add four great-spoonfuls of salt, one of pounded mace, half a table-spoonful of black pepper, a table-spoonful of powdered cloves, two table-spoonfuls of ground mustard, and a table-spoonful of celery seed tied in a muslin rag. Mix all and boil five or six hours, stirring frequently and constantly the last hour. Let it cool in a stone jar, take out the celery seed, add a pint of vinegar, bottle it and keep it in a dark, cool place.

XI.

FISH.

Stewed Oysters.—Strain off all the oyster liquor, and then add half as much water as you have oysters. Some of the best housekeepers say this is better than using the liquor. Add a salt-spoonful of salt for each pint of oysters, and half as much pepper; and when they begin to simmer, add half a small tea-cup of milk for each pint of oysters. When the edges begin to "ruffle," add some butter, and do not let them stand, but serve immediately. Oysters should not simmer more than five minutes in the whole. When cooked too long, they become hard, dark, and tasteless.

Fried Oysters.—Lay them on a cloth to absorb the liquor; then dip first in beaten egg, and afterward in powdered cracker, and fry in hot lard or butter to a light brown. If fresh lard is used, put in a little salt. Cook quickly in very hot fat, or they will absorb too much grease.

Oyster Fritters.—Drain off the liquor, and to each pint of oysters take a pint of milk, a salt-spoonful of salt, half as much pepper, and flour enough for thin batter. Chop the oysters and stir in, and then fry in hot lard, a little salted, or in butter. Drop in one spoonful at a time. Some make the batter thicker so as to put in one oyster at a time surrounded by the batter.

Scalloped Oysters.—Make alternate layers of oysters and crushed crackers wet with oyster liquor, and milk warmed. Sprinkle each layer with salt and pepper, (some add a *very* little nutmeg or cloves;) let the top and bottom layer be crackers. Put bits of butter on the top, pour on some milk with a beaten egg in it, and bake half an hour.

Broiled Oysters.—Dip in fine cracker crumbs, broil very quick, and put a small bit of butter on each when ready to serve.

Oyster Omelet, (very fine.)—Take twelve large oysters chopped fine. Mix the beaten yelks of six eggs into a tea-cupful of milk, and add the oysters. Then put in a spoonful of melted butter, and lastly add the whites of the eggs beaten to a stiff froth. Fry this in hot butter or salted lard, and do not stir it while cooking. Slip a knife around the edges while cooking, that the centre may cook equally, and turn it out so that the brown side be uppermost.

Pickled Oysters.—Take for fifty large oysters half a pint of vinegar, six blades of mace, twelve black pepper-corns, and twelve whole cloves. Heat the oysters with the liquor, but not to boil; take out the oysters, and then put the vinegar and spices into the liquor, boil it, and when the oysters are nearly cold, pour on the mixture scalding hot. Next day cork the oysters tight in glass jars, and keep them in a dark and cool place. Vinegar is sometimes made of sulphuric or pyroligneous acid, and this destroys the pickles. Use cider or wine vinegar.

Roast Oysters.—Put oysters in the shell, after washing them, upon the coals so that the flat side is uppermost, to save the liquor; and take them up when they begin to gape a little.

Scallops.—Dip them in beaten egg and cracker crumbs, and fry or stew them like oysters.

Clams.—Wash them and roast them; or stew or fry them like oysters; or make omelets or fritters by the recipe for oysters.

Clam Chowder.—Make alternate layers of crackers wet in milk, and clams with their liquor, and thin slices of fried salt pork. Season with black pepper and salt. Boil three quarters of an hour. Put this into a tureen, having drained off some liquor which is to be thickened with flour or pounded crackers, seasoned with catsup and wine, and then poured into the tureen. Serve with pickles.

Boiled Fish.—Wrap in a cloth wet with vinegar, floured inside. Boil in cold salted water till the bones will slip out easily; drain and serve with egg sauce, or drawn butter, or a sauce of milk, butter, and egg. Try boiling fish with a fork, and if that goes in easily, it probably is done.

Broiled Fish.—Split so that the backbone is in the middle; sprinkle with salt; lay the inside down at first till it begins to brown, then turn and broil the other side. Dress with butter, pepper, and salt. It is best to take out the backbone.

Baked Fish.—Wash and wipe, and rub with salt and pepper outside and inside. Set it on a grate over a baking-pan, and baste with butter and the drippings; if it browns too fast, cover with white paper. Thicken the gravy, and season to the taste, using lemon-juice or tomato catsup. Some put in wine.

Pickle for cold Fish.—To two quarts of vinegar add a pint of the liquor in which the fish was boiled, a dozen black pepper-corns, a dozen cloves, three sticks of cinnamon, and a tea-spoonful of mustard. Let them boil up, and then skim so as not to take out the spice.

Cut the fish into inch squares, and when the liquor boils, put them into it till just heated through. Pack tight in a glass jar, and then pour on the pickle; cook it till air-tight. This will keep a long time. It is a great convenience for a supper relish.

XII.

VEGETABLES.

FRESH-GATHERED vegetables are much the best. Soaking in cold water improves all. Always boil in *salted* water, a tea-spoonful for each quart of water. Do not let them stop boiling, or they will thus become watery.

POTATOES.

The excellence of potatoes depends greatly on the *species* and on the *age*. Much also depends on the cooking, and here there are diversities of modes and opinions. Peeling potatoes before cooking saves labor at the time of taking up dinner, which is a matter of consequence. They should, after peeling, soak an hour in cold water; then boil them in salted water, putting them in when the water boils. Have them equal in size, that all may be done alike. Try with a fork, and when tender drain off the water, sprinkle on a little fine salt, and set them in the oven, or keep them hot in the pot till wanted.

Some boil with skins on; in this case, pare off a small ring, or cut off a little at each end for the water within to escape, as this makes them more mealy.

Some make a wire basket and put in the potatoes peeled and of equal size; and when done, take them up and set in the oven a short time. This is the surest and easiest method.

Old potatoes should be boiled in salted water, then mashed with salt, pepper, and cream or butter.

New potatoes boil in salted water, and rub off the tender skins with a coarse towel.

A good Way for old Potatoes.—Peel and soak in cold water half an hour, then slice them into salted water that is boiling; when soft, pour off the water, add cream, or milk and butter, with salt and pepper, also dredge in a very little flour.

Another way is to chop the cold boiled potatoes, and then mix in milk, butter, salt, and pepper.

Some cold potatoes are nice cooked on a gridiron. A favorite relish for supper is cold potatoes sliced and dressed with a salad dressing of boiled eggs, salt, mustard, oil and vinegar.

Cold Potato Puffs.—Take cold mashed or chopped potatoes and stir in milk and melted butter. Beat two eggs and mix, and then bake till browned. It is very nice, and the children love it as well as their elders. This may be baked in patties for a pretty variety.

To cook Sweet Potatoes.—The best way is to parboil with the skins on, and then bake in a stove oven.

Green Corn.—Husk it; boil in salted water, and eat from the cob; or cut off the corn and season it with butter or cream and salt and pepper. If green corn is to be roasted, open it and take off the silk, and then cook it with husks on, buried in hot ashes; or if before the fire, turn it often.

Succotash.—Boil white beans by themselves. Cut the corn from the cob and let the cobs boil ten minutes, then take them out and put in the corn. Have only just water enough to cover the corn when cut. If there is more than a tea-cupful when the corn is boiled about half an hour, lessen it to that quantity, and add as much milk, and let the boiling continue till, on trial, the corn is soft, and then stir in a table-spoonful of flour wet in cold water. Then let it boil three or four minutes, take up the corn, and add the beans, with butter, pepper, and salt. Have twice as much corn as beans. Some use string-beans cut up.

If you have boiled corn left on the cob, cut it off for breakfast, and add milk and eggs, salt and pepper, and bake it. Some say this is the best way of all to cook sweet corn.

Salsify, or Oyster Plant.—Scrape, cut into inch pieces, and throw into cold water awhile; put into salted boiling water, just enough to cover them, and when tender turn off the water and add milk, butter, salt, and pepper, and thicken with a very little flour; then serve. Or, mash fine, and add a beaten egg and a little flour; make round, flat cakes, and cook on a griddle.

Egg Plant.—Cut into slices an inch thick and peel. Lay these in salted water an hour; then dip into egg, and rub in bread or cracker-crumbs, and cook on a griddle.

Carrots.—Boil in salted water till tender, take off the skin, slice and butter them. They are improved by cooking in broth. Some add chopped onion and parsley.

Beets.—Wash, but do not cut them before boiling; boil till tender, take off the skin, slice and season with salt, pepper, vinegar, and melted butter. If any are left, slice them into vinegar, for a pickle.

Parsnips.—Boil in salted water, take off the skins, cut in slices lengthwise, and season with salt, pepper, and butter. When cold, chop fine, add salt, pepper, egg, and flour, make small cakes, and cook on a griddle.

Pumpkin and Squash.—Cut in slices, boil in salted water till tender, drain, and season with salt, pepper, and butter. Baked pumpkin, cut in slices, is very good.

Celery.—Cut off the roots and green leaves, wash, and keep in cold water till wanted.

Radishes.—Wash, cut off tops, and lay in cold water till wanted.

Onions.—Many can not eat onions without consequent discomfort; though to most others they are a healthful and desirable vegetable. The disagreeable effect on the breath, it is said, may be prevented by afterward chewing and swallowing three or four roasted coffee-beans. Those who indulge in this vegetable should, as a matter of politeness and benevolence, try this precaution.

The best way to cook onions is to peel, cut off top and tail, put in cold water for a while, and then into boiling salted water. When nearly done, pour off the water, except a little, then add milk, butter, pepper, and salt.

When onions are old and strong, boil in two or three waters; have each time *boiling* water.

Tomatoes.—Pour on scalding water, then remove the skins, cut them up, and boil about half an hour. Add salt, butter or cream, and sugar. Adding green corn cut from the cob is a good variety. Some use pounded or grated stale bread-crumbs to thicken. Some slice without peeling, broil on a gridiron, and then season with pepper, salt, and butter. Some peel, slice, and put in layers, with seasoning and bread-crumbs between, and bake in an oven. If eaten raw, the skins should be removed by a knife, as scalding lessens flavor and crispness. Ice improves them much. The acid is so sharp that many are injured by eating too many.

Cucumbers.—Peel and slice into cold water, and in half an hour drain and season with salt, pepper, and vinegar. Some slice them quarter of an inch thick into boiling water, enough to cover them, and in fifteen minutes drain through a colander, and season with butter, salt, pepper and vinegar.

Cabbage and Cauliflower.—Take the outer leaves and look for any insects to be removed, and let it stand in cold water awhile. It should be cut twice transversely through the hardest part, that all may cook alike. It is more delicate if boiled awhile in one water then changed to another boiling hot water, in the same or another vessel. If you are cooking corned beef, use for the second water some of the meat liquor, and it improves the flavor. Drain it through a colander. Some chop the cabbage before serving, and add butter, salt, pepper, and vinegar. Others omit the vinegar, and add two beaten eggs and a little milk, then bake it like a pudding. This is the favorite mode in some families. Cauliflower is to be treated like cabbage.

Asparagus.—The best way to cook it is to cut it into inch pieces, leave out the hardest parts, boil in salted water, drain with a colander, and add pepper, salt, melted butter or cream, when taken up. Some beat up eggs and add to this, stir till hardened a little, and then serve.

Macaroni.—Break into inch pieces and put into salted boiling water, and stew till soft—say twenty minutes. Drain it and put it in layers in a pudding-dish, with grated cheese between each layer. Add a little salted milk or cream, and bake about half an hour. Many can not eat this with cheese. In this case it is better to pour cold soup or gravy upon it, and bake without cheese.

XIII.

FAMILY BREAD.

The most important article of food is good family bread, and the most healthful kind of bread is that made of coarse flour and raised with yeast. All that is written against the healthfulness of yeast is owing to sheer ignorance, as the most learned physicians and chemists will affirm.

Certain recent writers on hygiene are ultra and indiscriminating in regard to the use of unbolted flour. The simple facts about it are these: Every kernel of wheat contains nutriment for different parts of the body, and in about the right proportions. Thus, the outside part contains that which nourishes the bones, teeth, hair, nails, and the muscles. The germ, or eye, contains what nourishes the brain and nerves; and the central part (of which fine flour is chiefly made) consists of that which forms fat, and furnishes fuel to produce animal heat, while in gentle combustion it unites with oxygen in the capillaries. When first ground, the flour contains all the ingredients as in the kernel. The first bolting alters the proportions but very little, forming what is called *middlings*. The second bolting increases the carbonaceous proportion, making *fine* flour. The third bolting makes the superfine flour, and removes nearly all, except the carbonaceous portion, which is fitted only to form fat and generate animal heat. No animal could live on superfine flour alone but for a short time, as has been proved by experiments on dogs.

But meats, vegetables, fruit, eggs, milk, and several other articles in family diet contain the same elements as wheat, though in different proportions; so that it is only an *exclusive* use of fine flour that is positively dangerous. Still there is no doubt that a large portion of young children using white bread for common food, especially if butter, sugar, and molasses are added, have their teeth, bones, and muscles not properly nourished. And it is a most unwise, uneconomical, and unhealthful practice to use flour deprived of its most important elements because it is white and is fashionable. It would be much cheaper, as well as more healthful, to use the *middlings*, instead of fine or superfine flour. It would be still better to use unbolted flour, except where delicate stomachs can not bear it, and in that case the middlings would serve nearly as well for nutrition and give no trouble.

Some suppose that bread wet with milk is better than if wet with water, in the making. Many experienced housekeepers say that a little butter or lard in warm water makes bread that looks and tastes exactly like that wet with milk, and that it does not spoil so soon.

Experienced housekeepers say also that bread, *if thoroughly kneaded*, may be put in the pans, and then baked as soon as light enough, without the second or third kneading, which is often practiced. This saves care and trouble, especially in training new cooks, who thus have only one chance to make mistakes, instead of two or three.

It is not well to use yeast powders instead of yeast, because it is a daily taking of medicinal articles not needed, and often injurious. Cream tartar is supertartrate of potash, and soda is a supercarbonate of soda. These two, when united in dough, form tartrate of potash, tartrate of soda, and carbonate of soda; while some one of the three tends to act chemically and injuriously on the digestive fluids. Professor Hosford's method is objectionable for the same reason, especially when his medical articles are mixed with flour; for thus poor flour is sold more readily than in ordinary cases. These statements the best-informed medical men and chemists will verify.

Flour loses its sweetness by keeping, and this is the reason why sugar is put in the recipes for bread. The best kind of flour, when new and fresh ground, has eight per cent of sugar; and when such flour is used, the sugar may be omitted.

Some people make bread by mixing it so that it can be stirred with a spoon. But the nicest kind of bread can be made only with a good deal of kneading.

RECIPES FOR YEAST AND BREAD.

The best yeast is brewers' or distillery, as this raises bread much sooner than home-brewed. The following is the best kind of home-made yeast, and will keep good two or three weeks:

Hop and Potato Yeast.—Pare and slice five large potatoes, and boil them in one quart of water with a large handful of common hops, (or a square inch of pressed hops,) tied in a muslin rag. When soft, take out the hops and press the potatoes through a colander, and add a small cup of white sugar, a tea-spoonful of ginger, two tea-spoonfuls of salt, and two tea-cups of common yeast, or half as much distillery. Add the yeast when the rest is only blood-warm. White sugar keeps better than brown, and the salt and ginger help to preserve the yeast.

Do not boil in iron or use an iron spoon, as it colors the yeast. Keep yeast in a stone or earthenware jar, with a plate fitting well to the rim. This is better than a jug, as easier to fill and to cleanse. Scald the jar before making new yeast.

The rule for *quantity* is, one table-spoonful of brewers' or distillery yeast to every quart of flour; or twice as much home-made yeast.

Potato Yeast is made by the above rule, omitting the hops. It can be used in large quantities without giving a bitter taste, and so raises bread sooner. But it has to be renewed much oftener than hop yeast, and the bread loses the flavor of hop yeast.

Hard Yeast is made with home-brewed yeast, (not brewers' or distillery,) thickened with Indian meal and fine flour in equal parts, and then made into cakes an inch thick and three inches by two in size, dried in the wind but not in the sun. Keep them tied in a bag in a dry, cool place, where they will not freeze. One cake soaked in a pint of warm water, (not hot,) is enough for four quarts of flour. It is a good plan to work in mashed potatoes into this yeast, and let it rise well before using it. This makes the nicest bread. Some housekeepers say pour boiling water on one third of the flour, and then mix the rest in immediately, and it has the same effect as using potatoes.

When there is no yeast to start with, it can be made with one pint of new milk, one tea-spoonful of fine salt, and a table-spoonful of flour. When it is worked, use twice as much as common yeast. This is called Milk Yeast or Salt Risings, and bread made of it is poor, and soon spoils.

When yeast ceases to look foamy, and becomes watery, with sediment at the bottom, it must be renewed. When good, the smell is pungent, but not sour. If sour, nothing can restore it.

Bread of Fine Flour.—Take four quarts of sifted flour, one quart of lukewarm water, in which are dissolved two tea-spoonfuls of salt, two tea-spoonfuls of sugar, a table-spoonful of melted butter, and one cup of yeast. Mix and knead *very thoroughly*, and have it as soft as can be molded, using as little flour as possible. Make it into small loaves, put it in buttered pans, prick it with a fork, and when light enough to crack on the top, bake it. Nothing but experience will show when bread is just at the right point of lightness.

If bread rises too long, it becomes sour. This is discovered by making a sudden opening and applying the nose, and the sourness will be noticed as different from the odor of proper lightness. Practice is needed in this. If bread is light too soon for the oven, knead it awhile, and set it in a cool place. Sour bread can be remedied somewhat by working in soda dissolved in water—about half a tea-spoonful for each quart of flour. Many spoil bread by too much flour, others by not kneading enough, and others by allowing it to rise too much.

The goodness of bread depends on the quality of the flour. Some flour will not make good bread in any way. New and good flour has a yellowish tinge, and when pressed in the hand is adhesive. Poor flour is dry, and will not retain form when pressed. Poor flour is bad economy for it does not make as nutritious bread as does good flour.

Bread made with milk sometimes causes indigestion to invalids and to children with weak digestion.

Take loaves out of the pans, and set them sidewise, and not flat, on a table. Wrapping in a cloth makes the bread clammy.

Bread is better in small loaves. Let your pans be of tin, (or better, of iron,) eight inches long, three inches high, three inches wide at the bottom, and flaring so as to be four inches wide at the top. This size makes more tender crust, and cuts more neatly than larger loaves.

Oil the pans with a, swab and sweet butter or lard. They should be well washed and dried, or black and rancid oil will gather.

All these kinds of bread can be baked in biscuit-form; and, by adding water and eggs, made into griddle-cakes. Bread having potatoes in it keeps moist longest, but turns sour soonest.

Bread of Middlings or Unbolted Flour.—Take four quarts of coarse flour, one quart of warm water, one cup of yeast, two tea-spoonfuls of salt, one spoonful of melted lard or butter, two cups of sugar or molasses, and half a tea-spoonful of soda. Mix thoroughly, and bake in pans the same as the bread of fine flour. It is better to be kneaded rather than made soft with a spoon.

Bread raised with Water only.—Many persons like bread made either of fine or coarse flour and raised with water only. Success in making this kind depends on the proper quantity of water, quick beating, the heating of very small pans, and very quick baking. There are cast, iron patties made for this purpose, and also small, coarse earthen cups. The following is the rule, but it must be modified by trying:

Recipe.—To one quart of unbolted flour put about one quart, or a little less, of *hot* water. Beat it very quickly, put it in hot pans, and bake in a hot oven. White flour may be used in place of coarse, and the quantity ascertained by trial. When right, there is after baking little except a crust, which is sweet and crisp.

Rye and Indian Bread.—The Boston or Eastern Brown Bread is made thus: One quart of rye, one quart of corn-meal, one cup of molasses, half a cup of distillery yeast, or twice as much home-brewed; one tea-spoonful of soda, and one tea-spoonful of salt. Wet with hot water till it is stiff as can be stirred with a spoon. This is put in a large brown pan and baked four or five hours. It is good toasted, and improved by adding boiled squash.

Third Bread.—This is made with equal parts of rye, corn-meal, and unbolted flour. To one quart of warm water add one tea-spoonful of salt, half a cup of distillery or twice as much home-brewed yeast, and half a cup of molasses, and thicken with equal parts of these three kinds of flour. It is very good for a variety.

Rye Bread.—Take a quart of warm water, a tea-spoonful of salt, half a cup of molasses, and a cup of home brewed yeast, or half as much of distillery. Add flour till you can knead it, and do it very thoroughly.

Oat-Meal Bread.—Oat-meal is sometimes bitter from want of care in preparing. When good, it makes excellent and healthful bread.

Take one pint of boiling water, one great-spoonful of sweet lard or butter, two great-spoonfuls of sugar; melt them together, and thicken with two thirds oat-meal and one third fine flour. When blood-warm, add half a cup of home-brewed yeast and two well-beaten eggs. Mold into small cakes, and bake on buttered tins, or make two loaves.

Pumpkin Bread and Apple Bread.—These are very good for a variety. Stew and strain pumpkins or apples, and then work in either corn-meal or unbolted flour, or both. To each quart of the fruit add two table-spoonfuls of sugar, a pinch of salt, and a cup of home-brewed yeast. If the apples are quite sour, add more sugar. Make it as stiff as can be stirred with a spoon, and bake in patties or small loaves. Children like it for a change.

Corn-Meal Bread.—Always scald corn-meal. Melt two table-spoonfuls of butter or sweet lard in one quart of hot water; add a tea-spoonful of salt and a, tea-cup of sugar. Thicken with corn-meal, and one third as much fine flour, or unbolted flour, or middlings. Two well-beaten eggs improve it. Make it as stiff as can be easily stirred with a spoon, or, as some would advise, knead it like bread of white flour.

If raised with yeast, put in a tea-cup of home-brewed yeast, or half as much of distillery. If raised with powders, mix two tea-spoonfuls of cream tartar *thoroughly* with the meal, and one tea-spoonful of soda in the water.

Sweet Rolls of Corn-Meal.—Mix half corn-meal and half fine or unbolted flour; add a little salt, and then wet it up with sweetened water, raise it with yeast, and bake in small patties or cups in a very quick oven.

Soda Biscuit.—In one quart of flour mix *very thoroughly* two tea-spoonfuls of cream tartar, and a tea-spoonful of salt. Dissolve in a pint of warm water one tea-spoonful of soda and one table-spoonful of melted butter or lard. *Mix quickly;* add flour till you can roll, but let it be as soft as possible. Bake in a quick oven, and as soon as possible after mixing.

Yeast Biscuit.—Take a pint of raised dough of fine flour; pick it in small pieces; add one well-beaten egg, two great-spoonfuls of butter or lard, and two great-spoonfuls of sugar. Work thoroughly for ten minutes; add flour to roll, and then cut in round cakes and bake on tins, or mold into biscuits. Let them stand till light, and then bake in a quick oven.

If you have no dough raised, make biscuit as you would bread except adding more shortening.

Potato Biscuit.—Boil and press through a colander twelve *mealy* potatoes; any others are not good. While warm, add one cup of butter, one tea-spoonful of salt, four great-spoonfuls of sugar, and half a cup of yeast. Mix in white or coarse flour till it can be well kneaded. Mold into small cakes; let them stand till light, and bake in a quick oven. These are the best kind, especially if made of coarse flour.

Buns.—These are best made by the rule for potato biscuit, adding twice as much sugar. When done, rub over a mixture of half milk and half molasses, and it improves looks and taste.

XIV.

BREAKFAST AND SUPPER.

WHAT shall we have for breakfast to-morrow? is the constant question of trial to a housekeeper, and it is the aim of the present chapter to meet this want by presenting a good and successive variety of articles healthful, economical, and easily prepared.

Some of the best housekeepers have taken this method: they provide a good supply of the following articles, to be used in succession—rice, corn-meal, rye flour, wheat grits, unbolted wheat, cracked wheat, pearl wheat, oat grits, oat-meal, and hominy, with which they make a new article for every day in the week. Some one of these is selected for either a dinner vegetable or dessert, or for a dish at tea, and the remainder used for the next morning's breakfast.

The following will indicate the methods:

Corn-Meal.—Take four large cups of corn-meal, and scald it. In *all* cases, scald corn-meal before using it. Add half a cup of fine flour, three table-spoonfuls of sugar or molasses, one tea-spoonful of soda, and one of salt. Make a batter, and boil an hour or more, stirring often; or, better, cook in a tin pail set in boiling water. Use it as mush, with butter, sugar, and milk for supper. Next morning, thin it with hot water; add two or three eggs, and bake either as muffins or griddle-cakes.

Hominy.—Soak and then boil a quart of hominy with two heaping tea-spoonfuls of salt. Use it for dinner as a vegetable, or for supper with sugar and milk or cream. Next morning use the remainder, soaked in water or milk, with two eggs and a salt-spoonful of salt. Bake as muffins or griddle-cakes, or cut in slices, dipped in flour and fried. Farina may be used in the same way.

Rice.—Pick over one pint of rice; add two tea-spoonfuls of salt and three quarts of *boiling* water. Then boil fifteen minutes; then uncover; let it steam fifteen minutes. This to be used for a vegetable at dinner, or for a tea dish, with butter and sugar. At night, soak the remainder in as much milk or water, and next morning add as much fine or unbolted flour as there was rice, three eggs, a tea-spoonful of salt, and half a tea-spoonful of soda. Thin with water or milk, and bake as muffins or griddle-cakes.

The most economical Breakfast Dish, (healthful also.)—Keep a jar for remnants of bread, both coarse and fine, for potatoes, remnants of hominy, rice, grits, cracked wheat, oat-meal, and all other articles used on table. Add all remnants of milk, whether sour or sweet, and water enough to soak all, so as to be soft, but not thin. When enough is collected, add enough water to make a batter for griddle-cakes, and put in enough soda to sweeten it. Add two spoonfuls of sugar, and half a tea-spoonful of salt, and two eggs for each quart, and you make an excellent dish of material, most of it usually wasted. Thicken it a little with fine flour, and it makes fine waffles.

Biscuits of sour Milk and white or unbolted Flour.—One pint unbolted flour.
One spoonful of sugar.
One tea-spoonful of salt.
Melt a spoonful of butter in a little of the sour milk; then mix all, and just before setting in the oven, add very *quickly* and very *thoroughly* a tea-spoonful of soda dissolved in half a tea-cup of water. This should be done last and quickly, so that the carbonic acid gas produced by the union of the soda and the acid of the milk (lactic) may not escape. Use half a tea-cup of fine flour when molding into biscuits.

Pearl Wheat, or Cracked Wheat.—Boil one pint in a pail set in boiling water till quite soft, but so as not to lose its form. Add a tea-spoonful of sugar, and as much salt; also water, when needed. It must boil a long time. Eat a part for supper, with sugar and cream, and next morning add two eggs, a great-spoonful of sugar, and fine flour enough to make it suitable for muffin-rings or drop-cakes.

Rye and Corn-Meal.—Put into a pint and a half of boiling water one tea-spoonful of salt, two great-spoonfuls of sugar, two well-beaten eggs, three great-spoonfuls of corn-meal or unbolted wheat. Thicken with rye flour, and then add two well-beaten eggs. Bake in muffin-rings or as drop-cakes.

Oat-Meal.—Take one pint of boiling water, and pour it on to one pint of oat-meal. Add a great-spoonful of butter, half a tea-spoonful of salt, and two great-spoonfuls of sugar. Stir fast and thoroughly; then add two well-beaten eggs, and boil twenty minutes. To be eaten as mush for supper; and next morning thin it, and bake in muffin-rings.

Several of the above articles are good with only salt and water; and many persons would like them better with the butter, sugar, and eggs omitted.

Wheat Muffins.—One pint of milk, and two eggs.
One table-spoonful of yeast, and a salt-spoonful of salt. One table-spoonful of butter.
Mix these ingredients with sufficient flour to make a thick batter. Let it rise four or five hours, and bake in muffin-rings. This can be made of unbolted flour or grits, adding two great-spoonfuls of molasses, and it is very fine.
Make it so thick that a table-spoon will stand erect in it.

Sally Lunn improved.—Seven tea-cups of unbolted flour, or fine flour.
One pint of water.
Half a cup of melted butter, and half a cup of sugar.
One pinch of salt.
Three well-beaten eggs.
Two table spoonfuls of brewers' yeast, or twice as much of home-brewed.
Pour into square buttered pans, and let it rise two or three hours with brewers' yeast; with home-brewed, five hours are required. It is still better baked in patties.

Cream Griddle-Cakes.—One pint of thick cream.
One tea-spoonful of salt.
One table-spoonful of sugar.
Three well-beaten eggs.
Make a thin batter of unbolted or of fine flour, and bake on a griddle.

Royal Crumpets.—Three tea-cups of raised dough.
Two table-spoonfuls of melted butter.
Half a tea-cup of white sugar, mixed with three well-beaten eggs.
Bake in two buttered pans for half an hour.

Muffins of fine Flour or unbolted Flour.—One pint of milk or water.
One pinch of salt.
Two well-beaten eggs.
One table-spoonful of yeast.
Make a thick batter of fine flour or unbolted flour, and let it rise four or five hours. Bake in muffin-rings.

Unbolted Flour Waffles.—One pint of unbolted flour.
One pint of sour milk, or buttermilk, or water.
Half a tea-spoonful of soda, or more if needed, to sweeten the milk.
Three well-beaten eggs.
Two table-spoonfuls of sugar.

Drop-Cakes of fine Wheat or of Rye.—One pint of milk or water.
One pinch of salt.
Two table-spoonfuls of sugar.
Three well-beaten *eggs*.
Stir in rye, or fine or unbolted flour to a thick batter, and bake in cups or patties half an hour.

Sachem's Head Corn-Cake.—One quart of sifted corn-meal, scalded.
One tea-spoonful of salt.
Three pints of scalded sweet milk or water.
Half a tea-spoonful of soda in two great-spoonfuls of warm water.
Half a tea-cup of sugar.
Eight eggs, the whites beaten separately, and added the last thing.
Make the cakes an inch thick in buttered pans before baking, and, if baked right, they will puff up to double the thickness, like sponge-cake, and are very fine.

Rice Waffles.—One pint of milk. Half a tea-cup of solid boiled rice, soaked three hours in the milk.

Two cups of wheat flour or rice flour.

Three well-beaten eggs. Bake in waffle-irons.

The rice must be salted enough when boiled.

Another Rice Dish.—One pint of rice, well cleaned.

Three quarts of cold water.

Three tea-spoonfuls of salt.

Boil it twenty minutes; then pour off the water, add milk or cream, and let it boil ten minutes longer, till quite soft. Let it stand till cold, and then cut it in slices and fry it on a griddle. It can also be made into griddle-cakes or muffins by the preceding recipe.

A good and easy Way to use Cold Rice.—Heat a pint of boiled rice in milk: add two well-beaten eggs, a little salt, butter, and sugar; let it boil up once, and then grate on nutmeg.

Buckwheat-Cakes.—One quart of buckwheat.

One tea-spoonful of salt.

Two table-spoonfuls of distillery yeast, or four of home-brewed.

Two table-spoonfuls of molasses.

Wet the flour with warm water, and then add the other articles. Keep this warm through the night. If it sours, add half a tea-spoonful of soda in warm water. These cakes have a handsomer brown if wet with milk or part milk.

Fine Cottage Cheese.—Let the milk be turned by rennet, or by setting it in a warm place. It must not be *heated*, as the oily parts will then pass off, and the richness is lost. When fully turned, put in a coarse linen bag, and hang it to drain several hours, till all the whey is out. Then mash it fine, salt it to the taste, and thin it with good cream, or add but little cream, and roll it into balls. When thin, it is very fine with preserves or sugared fruit.

It also makes u fine pudding, by thinning it with milk, and adding eggs and sugar, and spice to the taste, and baking it. Many persons use milk when turned to *bonny-clabber* for a, dessert, putting on sugar and spice. Children are fond of it.

Various Ways of cooking Eggs.—Put eggs into boiling water from three to five minutes, according to taste. A hard-boiled egg is perfectly healthy if well masticated. Another way is to put them in a bowl or an egg-boiler, and pour on boiling water for two or three minutes, then pour off the water and add boiling water, and in five or six minutes the eggs will be cooked enough.

To make *plain omelet*, beat the yolks of six eggs, add a cup of milk, season with salt and pepper, and then stir in the whites cut to a stiff froth. Cook in a frying-pan or griddle, with as little butter or fat as possible. Let it cook about ten minutes, and then take up with a spad, or lay a hot dish over and turn the omelet on to it. This is improved by mixing in chopped ham or fowl. Some put sugar in, but it is more apt to burn.

A *bread omelet* is made as above, with bread-crumbs added, and is very good.

An *apple omelet* is made as above, with mashed apple-sauce added, and this also is very good. Jelly may be used instead of apple.

X.

PUDDINGS AND PIES.

Where sugar is made by slaves, the little children feed constantly on it, and grow fat and healthy. But they are nearly naked, live out of doors, exercise constantly, and have nothing to do but play. Thus their lungs and skin gain the healthful and purifying action of the air and the sun, and the excess of carbonaceous food is rendered harmless. But for those whose skin never meets the sun, rarely meets the air, and only now and then some water, a very different regimen is needful. Sugar, molasses, butter, and fats are chiefly carbonaceous, and, therefore, demand a large supply of oxygen through lungs and skin. And yet our custom is to use fine flour, which is chiefly carbon; butter and cream, chiefly carbon; sweet cakes, chiefly carbon; sweetmeats and candy, chiefly carbon; and worst of all, pie-crusts, chiefly carbon, and the most difficult of all food for digestion.

But the love for sweet food is common to all, and demands gratification. All that is required is moderation and temperance. For these reasons, a large supply is here provided of cakes and puddings, which are not rich, and yet are as highly relished as richer food. As pies are the most unhealthful of all food, some instruction and but few recipes are given, lest if entirely omitted, the book would not be read so widely, and other, more unhealthful ones be used.

The puddings here offered afford a great variety for desserts, are made with far less labor than pies, and are both more economical and more healthful. They also can be made more ornamental and attractive in appearance, and equally good to the taste. It is hoped, therefore, that the conscientious housekeeper will not tempt her family to eat unhealthful food when such an abundance is offered that is at once economical of labor time, expense, and health. The first recipe for pudding can be varied in many ways, and has the advantage which heretofore has recommended pies, namely, that several can be made at once, and kept on hand as equally good either cold or warmed over. It is also economical and convenient, as not requiring eggs or milk.

The Queen of all Puddings.—Soak a tea-cup of tapioca and a tea-spoonful of salt in three tumblerfuls of warm, not hot, water for an hour or two, till softened. Take away the skins and cores of apples without dividing them, put them in the dish with sugar in the holes, and spice if the apples are without flavor; not otherwise. Add a cup of water, and bake till the apples are softened, turning them to prevent drying, and then pour over the tapioca, and bake *a long time,* till all looks A BROWNISH YELLOW. Eat with a hard sauce. Do not fail to bake a long time.

This can be extensively varied by mixing chopped apples, or quinces, or oranges, or peaches, or any kind of berries with the tapioca; and then sugar must be added according to the acid of the fruit, though some would prefer it omitted when the sauce is used.

The beauty may be increased by a cover of sugar beaten into the whites of eggs, and then turned to a yellow in the oven. Several such puddings can be made at once, kept in a cool place, and when wanted warmed over; many relish it better when very cold. Sago can be used instead of tapioca. When no sago or tapioca are at hand, the following recipe for flour pudding may be used, baking long time:

Flour Puddings.—Take four table-spoonfuls of flour, half a tea-spoonful of salt, a pint of water or milk, three eggs, and a salt-spoonful of soda. Mix and beat very thoroughly, and bake as soon as done, or it will not be light. It must bake till the middle is not lower than the rest. Eat with liquid sauce. This can be cooked in a covered tin pan set in boiling water. This is enough for a family of five. Change the quantity according to the family.

This may be made richer by a spoonful of butter, more sugar, and some flavoring.

It will be lighter not to beat the eggs separately. If a bag is used to boil, rub flour or butter on the inside, to prevent sticking.

Flour and Fruit Puddings.—Add to the above, chopped apples or any kind of berries. Chopped apples and quinces together are fine when dried. When berries are used, a third more flour is needed for those very juicy, and less for cherries. Put in fruit the last thing.

Rusk and Milk.—Keep all bits of bread, dry in the oven, and pound them, putting half a salt-spoonful of salt to a pint. This eaten with good milk is what is especially relished by children, and named "rusk and milk."

Rusk Pudding's.— Mix equal quantities of rusk-crumbs with stewed fruit or berries, then add a *very sweet* custard, made with four or five eggs to a quart of milk. Eaten with sweet sauce. This may be made without fruit, and is good with sauce.

Meat and Rusk Pudding's.—Chop any kind of cold meat with salt pork or ham, season it well with butter, pepper, and salt, and add two or three beaten eggs. Then make alternate layers of wet rusk-crumbs, with milk or cold boiled hominy or rice, and bake half or three quarters of an hour. Let the upper layer be crumbs, and cover with a plate while baking, and, when nearly done, take it off to brown the top.

A handsome and good Pudding easily Made.—Put a pint of scalded milk (water will do as well) to a pint of bread-crumbs, and add the yelks of four eggs, well beaten, a tea-cup of sugar, butter the size of an egg, and the grated rind of one lemon. Bake and, when cool, cover with stewed fruit of any kind. Then beat the whites of the eggs into five table-spoonfuls of powdered sugar and the juice of one lemon. Cover the pudding with it, and set in the oven till it is a brownish yellow. Puddings covered with sugar and eggs in this way are called Meringue Puddings.

Pan Dowdy.—Put apples pared and sliced into a large pan, and put in an abundance of molasses or sugar, and some spice if the apples have little flavor; not otherwise. Cover with bread-dough, rolled thin, or a potato pie-crust. Bake a long time, and then break the crust into the fruit in small pieces. Children are very fond of this, especially if well sweetened and baked a long time.

Corn-Meal Pop-overs.—Two tumblers of scalded corn-meal fresh ground, three well-beaten eggs, a cap of milk or water, tea-spoonful of salt, and three of sugar, two spoonfuls of melted butter. Bake in hot patties, and eat with sweet sauce.

Best Apple-Pie.—Take a deep dish, the size of a soup-plate, fill it heaping with peeled tart apples, cored and quartered; pour over it one tea-cup of molasses, and three great-spoonfuls of sugar, dredge over this a considerable quantity of flour, enough to thicken the syrup a good deal. Cover it with a crust made of cream, if you have it; if not, common dough, with butter worked in, or plain pie-crust, lapping the edge over the dish, and pinching it down tight, to keep the syrup from running out. Bake about an hour and a half. Make several at once, as they keep well.

Rice Pudding.—One tea-cup of rice.
One tea-cup of sugar.
One half tea-cup of butter.
One quart of milk.
Nutmeg, cinnamon, and salt to the taste.
Put the butter in melted, mix all in a pudding-dish, and bake it two hours, stirring it frequently, until the rice is swollen.
This is good made without butter.

Bread and Fruit Pudding.—Butter a deep dish, and lay in slices of bread and butter, wet with milk, and upon these sliced tart apples, sweetened and spiced. Then lay on another layer of bread and butter and apples, and continue thus till the dish is filled. Let the top layer be bread and butter, and dip it in milk, turning the buttered side down. Any other kind of fruit will answer as well. Put a plate on the top, and bake two hours, then take it off and bake another hour.

Boiled Fruit Pudding.—Take light dough and work in a little butter, roll it out into a very thin large layer, not a quarter of an inch thick. Cover it thick with berries or stewed fruit, and put on sugar, roll it up tight, double it once or twice, and fasten up the ends. Tie it up in a bag, giving it room to swell. Eat it with butter, or sauce not very sweet.

Blackberries, whortleberries, raspberries, apples, and peaches, all make excellent puddings in the same way.

English Curd Pudding.—One quart of milk.
A bit of rennet to curdle it.

Press out the whey, and put into the curds three eggs, a nutmeg, and a table-spoonful of brandy. Bake it like custard.

Common Apple-Pie.—Pare your apples, and cut them from the core. Line your dishes with paste, and put in the apple; cover and bake until the fruit is tender. Then take them from the oven, remove the upper crust, and put in sugar and nutmeg, cinnamon or rose-water, to your taste. A bit of sweet butter improves them. Also, to put in a little orange-peel before they are baked, makes pleasant variety. Common apple-pies are very good to stew, sweeten, and flavor the apple before they are put into the oven. Many prefer the seasoning baked in. All apple-pies are much nicer if the apple is grated and then seasoned.

Plain Custard.—Boil half a dozen peach-leaves, or the rind of a lemon, or a vanilla bean in a quart of milk; when it is flavored, pour into it a paste made by a table-spoonful of rice flour, or common flour, wet up with two spoonfuls of cold milk and a half tea-spoonful of salt, and stir it till it boils again. Then beat up four eggs and put in, and sweeten it to your taste, and pour it out for pies or pudding. More eggs make it a rich custard.

Bake as pudding, or boil in a tin pail set in boiling water, stirring often, and pour into cups.

Another Custard.—Boil six peach-leaves, or a lemon-peel, in a quart of milk, till it is flavored; cool it, add three spoonfuls of sugar, a tea-spoonful of salt, and five eggs beaten to a froth. Put the custard into a tin pail, set it in boiling water, and stir it till cooked enough. Then turn it into cups; if preferred, it can be baked.

Mush, or Hasty Pudding.—Wet up the Indian-meal in cold water, till there are no lumps, stir it gradually into boiling water which has a little sugar and more salt added; boil till so thick that the stick will stand in it. Boil slowly, and so as not to burn, stirring often. Two or three hours' boiling is needed. Pour it into a broad, deep dish, let it grow cold, cut it into slices half an inch thick, flour them, and fry them on a griddle with a little lard, or bake them in a stove oven.

Stale Bread Pudding, (fine.)—Cut stale bread in thick slices, and put it to soak for several hours in cold milk.

Then cook on a griddle, with some salt, and eat it with sugar, or molasses, or a sweet sauce. To make it more delicate, take off the crusts. It is still better to soak it in uncooked custard. Baker's bread is best.

To prepare Rennet Wine.—Put three inches square of calf's rennet to a pint of wine, and set it away for use. Three table-spoonfuls will serve to curdle a quart of milk.

Rennet Custard.—Put three table-spoonfuls of rennet wine to a quart of milk, and add four or five great-spoonfuls of white sugar, and a salt-spoonful of salt. Flavor it with wine, or lemon, or rose-water. It must be eaten in an hour, or it will turn to curds.

Bird's-Nest Pudding.—Pare tart, well-flavored apples, scoop out the cores without dividing the apple, put them in a deep dish with a small bit of mace, and a spoonful of sugar in the opening of each apple. Pour in water enough to cook them. When soft, pour over them an unbaked custard, so as just to cover them, and bake till the custard is done.

A Minute Pudding of Potato Starch—Take four heaped table-spoonfuls of potato flour, three eggs, and tea-spoonful of salt, and one quart of milk. Boil the milk, reserving a little to moisten the flour. Stir the flour to a paste, perfectly smooth, with the reserved milk, and put it into the boiling milk. Add the eggs well beaten, let it boil till very thick, which will be in two or three minutes, then pour into a dish and serve with liquid sauce. After the milk boils, the pudding must be stirred every moment till done.

Tapioca Pudding.—Soak eight table-spoonfuls of tapioca in a quart of warm milk and tea-spoonful of sugar, till soft, then add two table-spoonfuls of melted sweet lard or butter, five eggs well beaten, spice sugar, and wine to your taste. Bake in a buttered dish, without any lining. Sago may be used in place of tapioca.

Cocoa-nut Pudding, (plain.)—Take one quart of milk, five eggs, and one cocoa-nut, grated. The eggs and sugar are beaten together, and stirred into the milk when hot. Strain the milk and eggs, and add the cocoa-nut, with nutmeg to the taste. Bake about twenty minutes like puddings.

New-England Squash or Pumpkin-Pie.—Take a pumpkin or winter-squash, cut in pieces, take off the rind and remove the seeds, and boil it until tender, then rub it through a sieve. When cold, add to it milk to thin it, and to each quart of milk five well-beaten eggs. Sugar, cinnamon, and ginger to your taste. The quantity of milk must depend upon the size and quality of the squash.

These pies require a moderate heat, and must be baked until the centre is firm.

Ripe Fruit-Pies—Peach, Cherry, Plum, Currant, and Strawberry.—Line your dish with paste. After picking over and washing the fruit carefully, (peaches must be pared, and the rest picked from the stem,) place a layer of fruit and a, layer of sugar in your dish, until it is well filled, then cover it with paste, and trim the edge neatly, and prick the cover. Fruit-pies require about an hour to bake in a thoroughly-heated oven.

Mock Cream.—Beat three eggs well, and add three heaping tea-spoonfuls of sifted flour. Stir it into a pint and a half of boiling milk, add a salt-spoon of salt, and sugar to your taste. Flavor with rose-water or essence of lemon.

This can be used for cream-cake's or pastry.

A Pudding of Fruit and Bread-Crumbs.—Mix a pint of dried and pounded bread-crumbs with an equal quantity of any kind of berries, or of dried and chopped sour apples. Add three eggs, half a pint of milk, three spoonfuls of fine flour, and half a tea-spoonful of salt. Bake on a griddle or in an oven in muffin-rings, or, when made thinner, as griddle-cakes. If dried fruit is used, more milk is needed than for fresh berries.

This may also be boiled for a pudding. Flour the pudding-cloth and tie tight, as it will not swell in cooking.

Bread and Apple Dumplings.—Mix half a pint of dried bread-crumbs and half a pint of fine flour. Wet it with water and two eggs thick enough to roll. Then put it around large apples peeled and cored whole, and boil for dumplings in several small floured cloths, or put all into one large floured cloth, tied tight, as they will not swell. Try with a fork, and when the apples are soft, take up and serve with a sweet sauce.

An excellent Indian Pudding without Eggs.—Take seven heaping spoonfuls of scalded Indian meal, half a tea-spoonful of salt, two spoonfuls of butter or sweet lard, a tea-cup of molasses, and two tea-spoonfuls of ginger or cinnamon, to the taste. Pour into these a quart of milk while boiling hot. Mix well and put in a buttered dish. Just as you set it in the oven, stir in a tea-cup of cold water, which will produce the same effect as eggs. Bake three quarters of an hour in a dish that will not spread it out thin.

Boiled Indian and Suet Pudding.—Three pints of milk, ten heaping table-spoonfuls of sifted Indian meal, a tumblerful of molasses, two eggs. Scald the meal with the milk, add the molasses and a tea-spoonful of salt. Put in the eggs when it is cool enough not to scald them. Put in a table-spoonful of ginger. Tie the bag so that it will be about two thirds full of the pudding in order to give room to swell. The longer it is boiled the better. Some like a little chopped suet with the above.

A Dessert of Rice and Fruit.—Pick over and wash the rice, and boil it fifteen minutes in water, with salt at the rate of a heaping tea-spoonful to u, quart. Rice is much improved by having the salt put in while cooking. Pour out the water in fifteen minutes after it begins to boil. Then pour in rich milk and boil till of a pudding thickness. Then pour it into cups to harden, when it is to be turned out inverted upon a platter in small mounds. Make an opening on the top of each and put in a pile of jelly or fruit. Lastly, pour over all a, custard made of three eggs, a pint of milk, and a tea-spoonful of salt boiled in a tin pail set in boiling water. This looks very prettily. Sweet cream with a little salt can be used instead of custard. This can be modified by having the whole put in a bowl and hardened, and then inverted and several openings made for the fruit.

Another Dessert of Rice and Fruit.—Boil the rice in salted water, a tea-spoonful to a quart of water. When cooked to a pudding consistency, cool it and then cut it in slices. Then put a thin layer of rice at the bottom of a pudding-dish, cover it with a thin layer of jelly or stewed fruit half an inch thick. Continue to add alternate layers of rice and jelly or fruit, smooth it at top, grate on sugar, and then cut the edges to show stripes of fruit and rice. Help it in saucers, and have cream or a thin custard to pour on it. Make the custard with two eggs, half a pint of milk, and half a tea-spoonful of salt. Boil it in a pail set in boiling water.

Dessert of Cold Rice and Stewed or Grated Apple.—Cut cold boiled rice in slices, and then lay in a buttered pudding-dish alternate layers of rice and grated or stewed apples. Add sugar and spice to each layer of apples. Cover with the rice, smooth with a spoon dipped in cold water or milk, and bake three quarters of an hour if the apples are raw. To be served with a sweet sauce.

A rich Flour Pudding.—Six eggs.
Three spoonfuls of flour.
One pint of milk.
A tea-spoonful of salt.

Beat the yelks well and mix them smoothly with the flour, then add the milk. Lastly, whip the whites to a stiff froth; work them in, and bake immediately.

To be eaten with a liquid sauce.

Apple-Pie.—Take fair apples; pare, core, and quarter them.
Take four table spoonfuls of powdered sugar to a pie.

Put into a preserving-pan, with the sugar; water enough to make a thin syrup; throw in a few blades of mace; boil the apple in the syrup until tender, a little at a time, so as not to break the pieces. Take them out with care, and lay them in soup-dishes.

When you have preserved apple enough for your number of pies, add to the remainder of the syrup cinnamon and rose-water, or any other spice, enough to flavor it well, and divide it among the pies. Make a good paste, and line the rim of the dishes, and then cover them, leaving the pies without an under crust. Bake them a light brown.

Spiced Apple Tarts.—Hub stewed or baked apples through a, sieve; sweeten them, and add powdered mace and cinnamon enough to flavor them. If the apples are not very tart, squeeze in the juice of a lemon. Some persons like the peel of the lemon grated into it. Line soup-dishes with a light crust, double on the rim, and fill them and bake them until the crust is done. Little bars of crust, a quarter of an inch in width, crossed on the top of the tart before it is baked, are ornamental.

Baked Indian Pudding.—Three pints of milk.
Ten heaping table-spoonfuls of Indian meal.
Three gills of molasses.
A piece of butter, as large as a hen's egg.
Scald the meal with the milk, and stir in the butter and molasses, and bake four or five hours. Some add a little chopped suet in place of the butter. This can be boiled.

Apple Custard.—Take half a dozen very tart apples, and take off the skin and cores. Cook them till they begin to be soft, in half a tea-cup of water. Then put them in pudding-dish, and sugar them. Then beat six eggs with four spoonfuls of sugar; mix it with three pints of milk, and two tea-spoonfuls of salt; pour it over the apples, and bake for about half an hour.

Plain Macaroni or Vermicelli Puddings.—Put two ounces of macaroni or vermicelli into a pint of milk, and simmer until tender. Flavor it by putting in two or three sticks of cinnamon while boiling, or some other spice when done. Then beat up three eggs, mix in an ounce of sugar, half a pint of milk, a tea-spoonful of salt, and a glass of wine. Add these to the broken macaroni or vermicelli, and bake in a slow oven.

Green Corn Pudding.—Twelve ears of corn, grated. Sweet-corn is best. One pint and a half of milk. Four well-beaten eggs. One tea-cup and a half of sugar.
Mix the above, and bake it three hours in a buttered dish. More sugar is needed if common corn is used.

Bread Pudding for Invalids or Young Children.—Grate half a pound of stale bread; add a pinch of salt, and pour on a pint of hot milk, and let it soak half an hour. Add two well-beaten eggs, put it in a covered basin just large enough to hold it, tie it in a pudding-cloth, and boil it half an hour; or put it in a buttered pan in an oven, and bake it that time. Make sauce of thin sweet cream, sweetened with sugar, and flavored with rose-water or nutmeg.

A Good Pudding.—Line a buttered dish with slices of wheat bread, first dipped in milk. Fill the dish with sliced apple, and add sugar and spice. Cover with slices of bread soaked in milk; cover close with a plate, and bake three hours.

Loaf Pudding.—When bread is too stale, put a loaf in a pudding-bag and boil it in salted water an hour and a half, and eat it with hard pudding sauce.

A Lemon Pudding.—Nine spoonfuls of grated apple, one grated lemon, (peel and pulp,) one spoonful of butter, and three eggs. Mix and bake, with or without a crust, about an hour. Cream improves it.

Green Corn Patties, (like oysters.)—Twelve ears of sweet-corn grated. (Yellow corn will do, but not so well.)

One tea-spoonful of salt, and one of pepper.

One egg beaten into two table-spoonfuls of flour.

Mix, make into small cakes, and cook on a griddle.

Cracker Plum Pudding, (excellent.)—Make a very sweet custard, and put into it a tea-spoonful of salt.

Take soda crackers, split them, and butter them very thick.

Put a layer of raisins on the bottom of a large pudding-dish, and then a layer of crackers, and pour on a little of the custard when warm, and after soaking a little, put on a thick layer of raisins, pressing them into the crackers with a knife. Then put on another layer of crackers, custard, and fruit, and proceed thus till you have four layers. Then pour over the whole enough custard to rise even with the crackers. It is best made over-night, so that the crackers may soak. Bake from an hour and a half to two hours.

During the first half-hour, pour on, at three different times, a little of the custard, thinned with milk, to prevent the top from being hard and dry. If it browns fast, cover with paper.

Bread and butter pudding is made in a similar manner.

SAUCES FOR PUDDINGS.

Liquid Sauce.—Six table-spoonfuls of sugar. Ten table-spoonfuls of water. Four table-spoonfuls of butter. Two table-spoonfuls of wine. Nutmeg, or lemon, or orange-peel, or rose-water, to flavor.

Heat the water and sugar very hot. Stir in the butter till it is melted, but be careful not to let it boil. Add the wine and nutmeg just before it is used.

Hard Sauce.—Two table-spoonfuls of butter.
Ten table-spoonfuls of sugar.

Work this till white, then add wine or grated lemon-peel, and spice to your taste.

Another Hard Sauce.—Mix half as much butter as sugar, and heat it fifteen minutes in a bowl set in hot water. Stir till it foams. Flavor with wine or grated lemon-peel.

A Healthful Pudding Sauce.—Boil, in half a pint of water, some orange or lemon-peel, or peach-leaves. Take them out and pour in a thin paste, made with two spoonfuls of flour, and boil five minutes. Then put in a pint of sugar, and let it boil. Then put in two spoonfuls of butter, add a glass of wine, and take it up before it boils.

An excellent Sauce for any kind of Pudding.—Beat the yelks of three eggs into sugar enough to make it quite sweet. Add a tea-cup of cream, or milk, and a little butter, and the grated peel and juice of two lemons. When lemons can not be had, use dried lemon-peel, and a little tartaric acid. This is a good sauce for puddings, especially for the starch minute pudding. Good cider in place of wine is sometimes used.

PASTE FOR PUDDINGS AND PIES.

This is an article which, if the laws of health were obeyed, would be banished from every table; for it unites the three evils—animal fat, *cooked* animal fat, and heavy bread. Nothing in the whole range of cooking is more indigestible than rich pie-crust, especially when, as bottom crust, it is made still wore by being soaked, or slack-baked. Still, as this work does; not profess to leave out unwholesome dishes, but only to set forth an abundance of healthful ones, and the reasons for preferring them, the best directions will be given for making the best kinds of paste.

Pie-Crusts without Fats.—Good crusts for plain pies are made by wetting up the crust with rich milk turned sour, and sweetened with saleratus. Still better crusts are made of sour cream, sweetened with saleratus.

Mealy potatoes boiled in salt water and mixed with the same quantity of flour, and wet with sour milk sweetened with saleratus, make a good crust.

Good light bread rolled thin makes a good crust for pan-dowdy, or pan-pie, and also for the upper crust of fruit-pies, to be made without bottom crusts.

Pie-Crust made with Butter.—Very plain paste is made by taking a quarter of a pound of butter for every pound of flour. Still richer, allows three quarters of a pound of butter to a pound of flour.

Directions for making rich Pie-Crust.—Take a quarter of the butter to be used, rub it thoroughly into the flour, and wet it with *cold* water to a stiff paste.

Next dredge the board thick with flour, cut up the remainder of the butter into thin slices, lay them upon the flour, dredge flour over thick, and then roll out the butter into thin sheets, and lay it aside.

Then roll out the paste thin, cover it with a sheet of this rolled butter; dredge on more, flour, fold it up and roll it out, and repeat the process till all the butter is used up.

Paste should be made as quick and as cold as possible. Some use a marble table in order to keep it cold. Roll *from* you every time.

XVI.

CAKE.

The multiplication of recipes for cakes, pies, puddings, and desserts is troublesome and needless, inasmuch as a little generalization will reduce them to a comparatively small compass, and yet afford a large variety.

Cake is of three classes, as raised either by eggs or by yeast or by powders; and different proportions of flour, sugar, shortening, and wetting make the variety, as appears in what follows.

GENERAL DIRECTIONS.

Sift flour, roll sugar, sift spices, and prepare fruit beforehand. Break eggs that are to be whipped, one at a time, in a cup, and let none of the yelk go in. Have them *cold*, and you will get on faster.

Excepting dough-cake, never use the hand in making cake, but a wooden spoon, and in an earthen vessel.

The goodness of cake depends greatly on baking. If too hot at bottom, set the pan on a brick; if too hot at top, cover with paper. If top-crust is formed suddenly, it prevents what is below from rising properly; and so, when the oven is very hot, cover with paper.

When fruit is used, sprinkle the fruit with a little flour to keep it from sinking when baking. Some put fruit in in layers, one in the middle and another near the top, as this spreads it evenly. Put in the flour just before baking.

When using whites beaten to a froth separately, put in the last thing, so that the bubbles of air which make the lightness may be retained more perfectly. Bake as soon as the cake is ready.

Water is as good as milk for most cakes as well as for bread; a mixture of new and stale milk injures the cake.

Streaks in cake are made either by imperfect mixing, or unequal baking, or by sudden decrease of heat before the cake is done. Try when cake is done, by inserting a splinter or straw; if it comes out clean, the cake is done.

The best way to keep cake is in a tin box or stone jar.

Do not wrap cake or bread in a cloth.

In baking, move cake *gently* if you change its place, or it will fall in streaks. Cake is more nicely baked when the pan is lined with oiled paper, especially in old pans, which often give a bad taste to the bottom and sides of the cake.

CAKE RAISED WITH POWDERS.

Although it is unhealthful to use powders in bread for daily food, the small quantity used for cake will do no harm.

The cake most easily made is raised with soda and cream tartar or other baking powders, and many varieties can be made by the following recipes:

One, Two, Three, Four Cake.—Take one cup of butter, (half a cup is better,) two caps of sugar, three cups of flour, and four eggs. Mix butter, sugar, and yelks. Then add the flour very thoroughly, and lastly the whites in a stiff froth. Bake immediately, and the cake will be light, with nothing added. But it is equally light to omit the eggs and work two tea-spoonfuls of cream tartar into the flour, and then mix well first the butter and sugar, and then the flour. When ready to bake, mix very thoroughly and quickly a tea-spoonful of soda, or a bit of sal volatile dissolved in a cup of warm (not hot) water. This makes two loaves. The following are varieties made by this recipe, using raising either with eggs or powders:

Chocolate-Cake.—Bake the above in thin layers, only a little thicker than carpeting. When nearly cool, spread over the cake a paste made of equal parts of scraped chocolate and sugar wet with water. Place the cake in layers one over another, frost the top, and then cut in oblong pieces for the cake-basket.

Jelly-Cake.—Proceed as above, only using jelly instead of chocolate.

Orange-cake.—Proceed as for jelly cake, having flavored the cake when making with a little grated orange-peel. The oranges must be peeled, chopped fine, and sweetened.

Almond and Cocoa-nut-Cake.—Blanch three ounces of almonds, (that is, pour on boiling water and take off the skins.) Chop or pound them with an equal quantity of sugar, make a thin paste with water, and use this instead of the jelly. Cocoa-nut, chopped fine, can be used instead of almonds. *Strawberries*, *Peaches*, *Cranberries*, and *Quinces*, and any other fruit, mashed or cooked, can be used in place of the jelly, being first sweetened.

This cake can be made richer by adding spices and fruit before baking. Those who have cream can use it in place of butter. Chopped almonds, citron, or cocoa-nut may be put *in* the cake for baking, making still another variety.

CAKE RAISED WITH EGGS.

Pound-Cake, (very rich.)—One pound of flour, one pound of sugar, half a pound of butter, nine eggs, a glass of brandy, one nutmeg, one tea-spoonful of pounded cinnamon. Mix half the flour with the butter, brandy, and spice; add the yelks of eggs beaten well into the sugar. Beat the whites to a stiff froth, and add them in alternate spoonfuls with the rest of the flour; then beat a long time, and bake as soon as done.

Plain Cake raised with Eggs.—Take a pound or quart of flour, half as much sugar, half as much butter as sugar, four or five eggs, one nutmeg, and a tea-spoonful of cinnamon. Mix well the sugar, butter, yelks, and spice; then the flour, and last the whites as stiff froth.

These two cakes are varied by adding citron, fruit, or other spices, making them more or less rich.

Fruit-Cake.—This to be made either like pound-cake, with fruit added; or like plain cake, raised with eggs or yeast, adding fruit.

Walnut-meats or *Almonds* may be chopped and put in the cake instead of fruit, making another variety.

Huckleberry-Cake.—One quart of huckleberries, three cups of sugar, three cups of flour, six eggs, one cup of sweet milk, and one tea-spoonful of soda dissolved in a little hot water. Cream the butter and sugar, and add the beaten yelks. Then add the milk, flour, and two grated nutmegs. Then add the whites, whipped to a stiff froth, and the berries, gently, so as not to mash them. An excellent cake.

Currants and other berries may be used in the same way. If very sour, add more sugar. If doubtful of raising it enough, add a tea-spoonful of soda; or, more surely, a bit of sal volatile the size of a hickory-nut.

Gold and Silver Cake.—This makes a pretty variety when cut and placed together in a cake-dish. For each, take one cup of sugar, (for the silver, white; and for the gold, brown,) half a cup of butter, half a cup of milk, two cups of flour, one tea-spoonful of cream tartar, and half as much soda. For the one, use the yelk of three eggs; and the white, as stiff froth, for the other. Mix the cream tartar very thoroughly in the flour, and put in the soda last. Bake immediately. This makes one loaf of each kind, in flat pans, and is to be frosted. If more is wanted, double the quantity of each ingredient.

Rich Sponge-Cake.—Take twelve eggs, and the weight of ten in sugar, and six in flour

Beat the sugar into the yelks, add the juice and grated peel of one lemon, then the flour, and then the whites cut to a stiff froth, and bake as soon as possible. Bake in brick-shaped pans, and line them with buttered paper.

Plain Sponge-Cake, (easily made.)—Mix thoroughly two cups of sifted flour and two cups of white sugar with one tea-spoonful of cream tartar. Beat four eggs to a froth, not separating the whites, and add some grated lemon-peel, or nutmeg, or rose-water. Just before baking, add half a tea-spoonful of soda dissolved in three great-spoonfuls of warm water. Beat quick, and set in the oven immediately.

GINGERBREAD, FRIED CAKES, COOKIES, AND OTHER CAKES.

Aunt Esther's Gingerbread.—Take half a pint of molasses, a small cup of soft butter, a gill and a half of water, a heaping tea-spoonful of soda dissolved in a table-spoonful of hot water, and one even table-spoonful of strong ginger, or two if weak. Rub butter and ginger into the flour, add the water, soda, and molasses, and while doing it, put in two table-spoonfuls of vinegar. Roll it in cards an inch thick, and bake half an hour in a quick oven.

Sponge Gingerbread.—Add to the above two beaten eggs, and water to make it thin as pound-cake, and bake as soon as well mixed.

Ginger-Snaps and Seed-Cookies.—One cup of butter, two cups of sugar or molasses, one cup of water, one table-spoonful of ginger, one heaping tea-spoonful of cinnamon and one of cloves, one tea-spoonful of soda dissolved in a small cup of hot water. Mix and add flour for a stiff dough, roll and cut in small round cakes. Omit the spices, and put in four or five table-spoonfuls of caraway seeds, and you have *seed-cakes* Leave out all spice and seeds, and you have plain cookies.

Fried Cakes.—For *doughnuts*, use the recipe for Plain Sponge-Cake, adding flour enough to roll. Or take Plain Cake raised with eggs, and add flour enough to roll. Or take Dough-Cake, or Plain Loaf-Cake, and thicken so as to roll. Roll about half an inch thick and cut into oblong pieces. For *crullers*, take plain cake raised with eggs, and thicken stiff with flour; roll it thin, and cut into strips, and form twisted cakes. More sugar and butter make it richer, but less healthful.

Have plenty of lard, or, better, strained beef-fat, quite hot; try with a small piece first, and, if right, there will be a bubbling. Turn two or three times to cook all alike, break open one to try if done, and when done, take up with a skimmer and drain well. If the fat is too hot, it will brown too quick; if not hot enough, the fat will soak into the cake. Remember that frying is the most unhealthful mode of cooking food, and the one most likely to be done amiss.

CAKE RAISED WITH YEAST.

Plain Loaf-Cake.—Two pounds of dried and sifted flour, a pint of warm water in which is melted a quarter of a pound of butter, half a tea-spoonful of salt, three eggs without beating, and three quarters of a pound of sugar, well mixed; and then add two nutmegs, two tea-spoonfuls of cinnamon, and two gills of home-brewed or half as much distillery yeast. When light, add two or three pounds of fruit, and let it stand half an hour.

Rich Loaf-Cake is made like the above, only adding more butter and sugar. The following are specimens of the diverse proportions: Four pounds of flour, three of sugar, two of butter, a quart of water or milk, ten unbeaten eggs, half a pint of wine, three nutmegs, three tea-spoonfuls of cinnamon, and two cloves; two gills of distillery yeast, or twice as much home-brewed. This is what in New-England would be called Election or Commencement-Cake. Two or three risings used to be practiced, but one is as good if the mixing is thorough.

Dough-Cake.—Three cups of raised dough, half a cup of butter, two cups of sugar, two eggs, fruit and spice to the taste. When light, bake in loaves. This can be made more or less sweet and shortened by lessening or increasing the quantity of dough. It must be mixed with the hands.

Icing for Cake.—Put the whites of eggs into a dish, and for each egg use about a quarter of a pound of sugar. Beat the whites, slowly adding the sugar. This is better than beating the whites first, and then adding sugar. A little lemon-juice or tartaric acid makes it whiter and better. Spread the icing, after pouring it upon the centre, with a knife dipped in water. If you can, dry in an open, sunny window. Otherwise, harden it in the oven. It improves it by mixing, when adding sugar, some almonds pounded to a thin paste.

XVII.

PRESERVES AND JELLIES.

General Directions.

GATHER fruit when it is dry.

Long boiling hardens the fruit.

Pour boiling water over the sieves used, and wring out jelly-bags in hot water the moment you are to use them.

Do not squeeze while straining through jelly-bags.

Let the pots and jars containing sweetmeats just made, remain uncovered three days.

For permanent covering, lay brandy papers over the top, cover them tight, and seal them; or, what is best of all, soak a split bladder and tie it tight over them. In drying, it will shrink so as to be perfectly air-tight.

Keep them in a dry but not warm place.

A thick, leathery mold helps to preserve fruit, but when mold appears in specks, the preserves must be scalded in a warm oven, or the jars containing them are to be set into hot water which must then boil till the preserves are scalded.

Always keep watch of preserves which are not sealed, especially in warm and damp weather. The only sure way to keep them without risk or care is to make them with enough sugar and seal them or tie bladder covers over.

The best kettle is iron lined with porcelain. If brass is used, it must be bright, or acids will make a poison.

The chief art is to boil continuously, slowly, and gently, and take up as soon as done; too long boiling makes the fruit hard and dark. Jellies will not harden well if the boiling stops for some minutes. Try jellies with a spoon, and as soon as they harden around the edge quickly, they are done. In making, the sugar should be heated and not added till the juice boils.

Keep preserves in small glass jars, as frequent opening injures them.

Canned Fruit.—This is far more economical than to preserve in sugar. Some can be canned without any sugar, and very nice sugar demands only one fourth sugar to three fourths fruit. The best cans are glass with metal tops. Those of Wilcox are the best known to the author. The W. L. Imlay's of Philadelphia are recommended as best of any.

Directions.—Set the jars in a large boiler, and then fill it with cold water and heat to boiling. Having filled the jars to within an inch of the top with alternate layers of fruit and sugar, (in proportion of one half or one fourth of a pound of sugar to a pound of fruit, according as it is more or less acid,) set them in cold water. As soon as the fruit has risen to the top of the jar, screw on the cover and take from the water. Peaches and pears may be canned without sugar.

To clarify Syrup for Sweetmeats.—For each pound of sugar allow half a pint of water. For every three pounds of sugar allow the white of one egg. Mix when cold, boil a few minutes, and skim it. Let it stand ten minutes and skim it again, then strain it.

Brandy Peaches.—Prick the peaches with a needle, put them into kettle with cold water, heat the water, scald them until sufficiently soft to be penetrated with a straw. Take half a pound of sugar to every pound of peaches; make the syrup with the sugar, and while it is a little warm mix two thirds as much of white brandy with it, put the fruit into jars and pour the syrup over it. The late white clingstones are the best to use.

Peaches, (not very rich.)—To six pounds of fruit put five of sugar. Make the syrup. Boil the fruit in the syrup till it is clear. If the fruit is ripe, half an hour will cook it sufficiently.

Peaches, (very elegant.)—First take out the stones, then pare them. To every pound of peaches allow one third of a pound of sugar. Make a thin syrup, boil the peaches in the syrup till tender, but not till they break. Put them into a bowl and pour the syrup over them. Put them in a dry, cool place and let them stand two days. Then make a new, rich syrup, allowing three quarters of a pound of sugar to one of fruit. Drain the peaches from the first syrup, and boil them until they are clear in the last syrup. The first syrup must not be added, but may be used for any other purpose you please, as it is somewhat bitter. The large white clingstones are the best.

To preserve Quinces whole.—Select the largest and fairest quinces, (as the poorer ones will answer for jelly.) Take out the cores and pare them. Boil the quinces in water till tender. Take them out separately on a platter. To each pound of quince allow a pound of sugar. Make the syrup, then boil the quinces in the syrup until clear.

Quince Jelly.—Rub the quinces with a cloth until perfectly smooth. Remove the cores, cut them into small pieces, pack them tight in your kettle, pour cold water on them until it is on a level with the fruit, but not to cover it; boil till very soft, but not till they break. Dip off all the liquor you can, then put the fruit into a sieve and press it, and drain off all the remaining liquor. Then to a pint of the liquor add a pound of sugar and boil it fifteen minutes Pour it, as soon as cool, into small jars or tumblers. Let it stand in the sun a few days, till it begins to dry on the top. It will continue to harden after it is put up.

Calf's Foot Jelly.—To four nicely cleaned calf's feet put four quarts of water; let it simmer gently till reduced to two quarts, then strain it and let it stand all night. Then take off all the fat and sediment, melt it, add the juice, and put in the peel of three lemons and a pint of wine, the whites of four eggs, three sticks of cinnamon, and sugar to your taste. Boil ten minutes, then skim out the spice and lemon-peel and strain it.

The American gelatine, now very common, makes as good jelly, with far less trouble; and in using it, you only need to dissolve it in hot water, and then sweeten and flavor it.

To preserve Apples.—Take only tart and well-flavored apples; peel and take out the cores without dividing them, and then parboil them. Make the syrup with the apple water, allowing three quarters of a pound of white sugar to every pound of apples, and boil some lemon-peel and juice in the syrup. Pour the syrup, while boiling, upon the apples, turn them gently while cooking, and only let the syrup simmer, as hard boiling breaks the fruit. Take it out when the apple is tender through. At the end of a week, boil them once more in the syrup.

Pears.—Take out the cores, cut off the stems, and pare them. Boil the pears in water till they are tender. Watch them that they do not break. Lay them separately on a platter as you take them out. To each pound of fruit take a pound of sugar. Make the syrup, and boil the fruit in the syrup till clear.

Pineapples, (very fine.)—Pare and *grate* the pineapple. Take an equal quantity of fruit and sugar. Boil them slowly in a sauce-pan for half an hour.

Purple Plums, No. 1.—Make a rich syrup. Boil the plums in the syrup very gently till they begin to crack open. Then take them from the syrup into a jar, and pour the syrup over them. Let them stand a few days, and then boil them a second time very gently.

Purple Plums, No. 2.—Take an equal weight of fruit and nice brown sugar. Take a clean stone jar, put in a layer of fruit and a layer of sugar till all is in. Cover them tightly with dough, or other tight cover, and put them in a brick oven after you have baked in it. If you bake in the morning, put the plums in the oven at evening, and let them remain till the next morning. When you bake again, set them in the oven as before. Uncover them and stir them carefully with a spoon, and so as not to break them. Set them in the oven thus *the third* time, and they will be sufficiently cooked.

White or Green Plums.—Put each one into boiling water and rub off the skin. Allow a pound of fruit to a pound of sugar. Make a syrup of sugar and water. Boil the fruit in the syrup until clear—about twenty minutes. Let the syrup be cold before you pour it over the fruit. They can be preserved without taking off the skins by pricking them. Some of the kernels of the stones boiled in give a pleasant flavor

Citron Melons.—Two fresh lemons to a pound of melon. Let the sugar be equal in weight to the lemon and melon. Take out the pulp of the melon and cut it in thin slices, and boil it in fair water till tender. Take it out and boil the lemon in the same water about twenty minutes. Take out the lemon, add the sugar, and, if necessary, a little more water. Let it boil. When clear, add the melon and let it boil a few minutes.

Strawberries.—Look over them with care. Weigh a pound of sugar to each pound of fruit. Put a layer of fruit on the bottom of the preserving-kettle, then a layer of sugar, and so on till all is in the pan. Boil them about fifteen minutes. Put them in bottles, hot, and seal them. Then put them in a box and fill it in with dry sand. The flavor of the fruit is preserved more perfectly by simply packing the fruit and sugar in alternate layers, and sealing the jar, without cooking; but the preserves do not look so well.

Blackberry Jam.—Allow three quarters of a pound of brown sugar to a pound of fruit. Boil the fruit half an hour, then add the sugar and boil all together ten minutes.

To preserve Currants to eat with Meat.—Strip them from the stem. Boil them an hour, and then to a pound of the fruit add a pound of brown sugar. Boil all together fifteen or twenty minutes.

Cherries.—Take out the stones. To a pound of fruit allow a pound of sugar. Put a layer of fruit on the bottom of the preserving-kettle, then a layer of sugar, and continue thus till all are put in. Boil till clear. Put them in bottles hot and seal them. Keep them in dry sand.

Currants.—Strip them from the stems. Allow a pound of sugar to a pound of currants. Boil them together ten minutes. Take them from the syrup and let the syrup boil twenty minutes, and pour it on the fruit. Put them, in small jars or tumblers, and let them stand in the sun a few days.

Raspberry Jam, No. 1.—Allow a pound of sugar to a pound of fruit. Press them with a spoon in an earthen dish. Add the sugar, and boil all together fifteen minutes.

Raspberry Jam, No. 2.—Allow a pound of sugar to a pound of fruit. Boil the fruit half an hour or till the seeds are soft. Strain one quarter of the fruit and throw away the seeds. Add the sugar and boil the whole ten minutes. A little currant-juice gives it a pleasant flavor, and when that is used, an equal quantity of sugar must be added.

Currant Jelly.—Pick over the currants with care. Put them in a stone jar, and set it into a kettle of boiling water. Let it boil till the fruit is very soft. Strain it through a sieve. Then run the juice through a jelly-bag. Put a pound of sugar to a pint of juice, and boil it together five minutes. Set it n the sun a few days. If it stops boiling, it is less likely to turn to je

Quince Marmalade.—Rub the quinces with a cloth, cut them in quarters. Put them on the fire with a little water, and stew them till they are sufficiently tender to rub them through a sieve. When strained, put a pound of sugar to a pound of the pulp. Set it on the fire, and let it cook slowly. To ascertain when it is done, take out a little and let it get cold, and if it cuts smoothly, it is done.

Crab-apple marmalade is made in the same way.

Crab-apple jelly is made like quince jelly.

Most other fruits are preserved so much like the preceding that it is needless to give any more particular directions than to say that a pound of sugar to a pound of fruit is the general rule for all preserves that are to be kept through warm weather and a long time.

Preserved Watermelon Rinds.—This a fine article to keep well without trouble for a long time. Peel the melon, and boil it in just enough water to cover it till it is soft, trying with a fork. (If you wish it green, put green vine-leaves above and below each layer, and scatter powdered alum, less than half a tea-spoonful to each pound.)

Allow a pound of sugar to each pound of rind, and clarify it as directed previously.

Simmer the rinds two hours in this syrup, and flavor it with lemon-peel grated and tied in a bag. Then put the melon in a tureen, and boil the syrup till it looks thick, and pour it over. Next day, give the syrup another boiling, and put the juice of one lemon to each quart of syrup. Take care not to make it bitter by too much of the peel.

Citrons are preserved in the same manner. Both these keep through hot weather with very little care in sealing and keeping.

XVIII.

DESSERTS AND EVENING PARTIES.

Ice-Cream.—One quart of milk. One and half table-spoonfuls of arrowroot. The grated peel of two lemons. One quart of thick cream.

Wet the arrow-root with a little cold milk, and add it to the quart of milk when boiling hot sweeten it very sweet with white sugar, put in the grated lemon-peel, boil the whole, and strain it into the quart of cream. When partly frozen, add the juice of the two lemons. Twice this quantity is enough for thirty-five persons. Find the quantity of sugar that suits you by measure, and then you can use this every time, without tasting. Some add whites of eggs; others think it just as good without. It must be made *very* sweet, as it loses much by freezing.

If you have no apparatus for freezing, (which is *almost* indispensable,) put the cream into a tin pail with a very tight cover, mix equal quantities of snow and blown salt, (not the coarse salt,) or of pounded ice and salt, in a tub, and put it *as high as the pail, or freezer;* turn the pail or freezer half round and back again with one hand, for half an hour, or longer, if you want it very nice. Three quarters of an hour steadily will make it good enough. While doing this, stop four or five times, and mix the frozen part with the rest, the last time very thoroughly, and then the lemon juice must be put in. Then cover the freezer tight with snow and salt till it is wanted. The mixture must be perfectly cool before being put in the freezer. Renew the snow and salt while shaking, so as to have it kept tight to the sides of the freezer. A hole in the tub holding the freezing mixture, to let off the water, is a great advantage. In a tin pail it would take much longer to freeze than in the freezer, probably nearly twice as long. A long stick, like a coffee-stick, should be used in scraping the ice from the sides. Iron spoons will be affected by the lemon-juice, and give a bad taste.

In taking it out for use, first wipe off every particle of the freezing mixture dry, then with a knife loosen the sides, then invert the freezer upon the dish in which the ice is to be served, and apply two towels wrung out of hot water to the bottom part, and the whole will slide out in the shape of a cylinder. Freezers are now sold quite cheap, and such as freeze in a short time.

Strawberry Ice-Cream.—Rub pint of ripe strawberries through a sieve, add a pint of cream, and four ounces of powdered sugar, and freeze it. Otber fruits may be used thus.

Ice-Cream without Cream.—A vanilla bean or a lemon rind is first boiled in a quart of milk. Take out the bean or peel, and add the yelks of four eggs, beaten well. Heat it scalding hot, but do not boil it, stirring in white sugar till *very* sweet. When cold, freeze it.

Fruit Ice-Cream.—Make rich boiled custard, and mash into it the soft ripe fruit, or the grated or cooked hard fruit, or grated pine-apples. Rub all through a sieve, sweeten it very sweet, and freeze it. Quince, apple, pear, peach, strawberry, and raspberry are all very good for this purpose.

A Cream for stewed Fruit.—Boil two or three peach leaves, or vanilla bean, in a quart of cream, or milk, till flavored. Strain and sweeten it, mix it with the yelks of four eggs, well beaten; then, while heating it, add the whites cut to a froth. When it thickens, take it up When cool, pour it over the fruit or preserves.

Currant, Raspberry, or Strawberry Whisk.—Put three gills of the juice of the fruit to ten ounces of crushed sugar, add the juice of a lemon, and a pint and a half of cream. Whisk it till quite thick, and serve it in jelly-glasses or a glass dish.

Lemonade Ice, and other Ices.—To a quart of lemonade, add the whites of six eggs, cut to a froth, and freeze it. The juices of any fruit, sweetened and watered, may be prepared in the same way, and are very fine.

Charlotte Russe.—One ounce of gelatine simmered in half a pint of milk or water, four ounces of sugar beat into the yelks of four eggs, and added to the gelatine when dissolved. Then add a pint of cream or new milk. Lastly, add the whites beat to a stiff froth, and beat all together. Line a mold with slices of sponge-cake and set it on ice, and when the cream is a little thickened, fill the mould; let it stand five or six hours, and then turn it into a dish.

Flummery.—Cut sponge-cake into thin slices, and line a deep dish. Make it moist with white wine; make rich custard, using only the yelks of the eggs. When cool, turn it into the dish, and cut the whites to a stiff froth, and put on the top.

Chicken Salad.—Cut the white meat of chickens into small bits the size of peas. Chop the white parts of celery nearly as small.

Prepare a dressing thus: rub the yelks of hard-boiled eggs smooth, to each yelk put half a tea-spoonful of liquid mustard, the same quantity of salt, a table-spoonful of oil mixed in very slowly and thoroughly, and half a wine-glass of vinegar. Mix the chicken and celery in a large bowl, and pour over this dressing.

The dressing must not be put on till just before it is used. Bread and butter and crackers are served with it.

Wine Jelly.—Two ounces of American isinglass or gelatine. One quart of boiling water. A pint and a half of white wine. The whites of three eggs.

Soak the gelatine in cold water half an hour Then take it from the water, and pour on the quart of boiling water. When cooled, add the grated rind of one lemon, and the juice of two, and a pound and a half of loaf-sugar. Then beat the whites of the eggs to a stiff froth, and stir them in, and let the whole boil till the egg is well mixed, but do not stir while it boils. Strain through a jelly-bag, and then add the wine.

In cold weather, a pint more of water may be added. This jelly can be colored by beet-juice, saffron, or indigo, for fancy dishes.

An Apple Lemon Pudding.—Six spoonfuls of grated, or of cooked and strained, apple. Three lemons, pulp, rind, and juice, all grated. Half a pound of melted butter. Sugar to the taste. Seven eggs well beaten.

Mix, and bake with or without paste. It can be made still plainer by using nine spoonfuls of apple, one lemon, two thirds of a cup full of butter, and three eggs.

Wheat Flour Blane-Mange.—Wet up six table-spoonfuls of flour to a thin paste with cold milk, and stir it into a pint of boiling milk. Flavor with lemon-peel or peach-leaves boiled in the milk. Add a pinch of salt, cool it in a mold, and eat with sweetened cream and sweetmeats.

Orange Marmalade.—Take two lemons and a dozen oranges; grate the yellow rinds of all the oranges but five, and set it aside. Make a clear syrup of an equal weight of sugar. Clear the oranges of rind and seeds, put them with the grated rinds into the syrup, and boil about twenty minutes till it is a transparent mass.

A simple Lemon Jelly, (easily made.)—One ounce of gelatine. A pound and a half of loaf-sugar. Three lemons, pulp, skin, and juice, grated.

Pour a quart of boiling water upon the isinglass, add the rest, mix and strain it, then add a glass of wine, and pour it to cool in some regular form. If the lemons are not fresh, add a little cream of tartar or tartaric acid.

Cranberry.—Pour boiling water on them, and then you can easily separate the good and the bad. Boil them in a, very little water till soft then sweeten to your taste. If you wish a jelly, take a portion and strain through a fine sieve.

Apple Ice, (very fine.)—Take finely-flavored apples, grate them fine, and then make them *very* sweet, and freeze them. It is very delicious.

Pears, peaches, or quinces also are nice, either grated fine or stewed and run through a sieve, then sweetened very sweet, and frozen. The flavor is much better preserved when grated than when cooked.

Whip Syllabub.—One pint of cream. Sifted white sugar to your taste. Half a tumbler of white wine. The grated rind and juice of one lemon. Beat all to a stiff froth.

Apple Snow.—Put six very tart apples in cold water over a slow fire. When soft, take away the skins and cores, and mix in a pint of sifted white sugar; beat the whites of six eggs to stiff froth, and then add them to the apples and sugar. Put it in a dessert-dish and ornament with myrtle and box.

Iced Fruit.—Take fine bunches of currants on the stalk, dip them in well-beaten whites of eggs, lay them on a sieve and sift white sugar over them, and set them in a warm place to dry.

Ornamental Froth.—The whites of four eggs in a stiff froth, put into the syrup of preserved raspberries or strawberries, beaten well together, and turned over ice-cream or blanc-mange. Make white froth to combine with the colored in fanciful ways. It can be put on the top of boiling milk, and hardened to keep its form.

To clarify Isinglass.—Dissolve an ounce of isinglass in a cup of boiling water, take off the scum, and drain through a coarse cloth. Jellies, candies, and blanc-mange should be done in brass and stirred with silver.

Blanc-Mange.—Two and a half sheets of gelatine broken into one quart of milk; put in a warm place and stir till it dissolves. An ounce and a half of clarified isinglass stirred into the milk. Sugar to your taste. A tea-spoonful of fine salt. Flavor with lemon, or orange, or rose-water. Let it boil, stirring it well, then strain it into molds.

Three ounces of almonds pounded to a paste and added while boiling is an improvement. Or filberts or hickory-nuts can be skinned and used thus. It can be flavored by boiling in it a vanilla bean or a stick of cinnamon. (Save the bean to use again.)

Apple Jelly.—Boil tart peeled apples in a little water till glutinous; strain out the juice, and put a pound of white sugar to a pint of the juice. Flavor to your taste, boil till a good jelly, and then put it into molds.

Orange Jelly.—The juice of nine oranges and three lemons. The grated rind of one lemon, and one orange, pared thin. Two quarts of water, and four ounces of gelatine broken up and boiled in it to a jelly. Add the above, and sweeten to your taste. Then add the whites of eight eggs, well beaten to a stiff froth, and boil ten minutes; strain and put into molds, first dipped in cold water. When perfectly cold, dip the mold in warm water, and turn on to a glass dish.

Floating Island.—Beat the yelks of six eggs with the juice of four lemons, sweeten it to your taste, and stir it into a quart of boiling milk till it thickens, then pour it into a dish. Whip the whites of the eggs to a stiff froth, and put it on the top of the cream.

A Dish of Snow.—Grate the white part of cocoa-nut, put it in a glass dish and serve with, oranges sliced and sugared, or with currant or cranberry jellies.

To clarify Sugar.—Take four pounds of sugar, and break it up. Whisk the white of an egg, and put it with a tumblerful of water into a preserving-pan, and add water gradually till you have two quarts, stirring well. When there is a good frothing, throw in the sugar, boil moderately, and skim it. If the sugar rises to run over, throw in a little cold water, and then skim it, as it is then still. Repeat this, and when no more scum rises, strain the sugar for use.

Candied Fruits.—Preserve the fruit, then dip it in sugar boiled to candy thickness, and then dry it. Grapes and some other fruits may be dipped in uncooked, and then dried, and they are fine.

Another Way.—Take it from the syrup, when preserved, dip it in powdered sugar, and set it on a sieve in an oven to dry.

To make an Ornamental Pyramid for a Table.—Boil loaf-sugar as for candy, and rub it over a stiff form made for the purpose, of stiff paper or pasteboard, which must be well buttered. Set it on a table, and begin at the bottom, and stick on to this frame with the sugar, a row of macaroons, kisses, or other ornamental articles, and continue till the whole is covered. When cold, draw out the pasteboard form, and set the pyramid in the centre of the table with a small bit of wax candle burning with it, and it looks very beautifully.

XIX.

DRINKS AND ARTICLES FOR THE SICK AND YOUNG CHILDREN.

Drinks made of the juice of fruits and water are good for all who are in health. Various preparations of cocoa-nuts are so also. Tea is often made or adulterated with unhealthful articles. Coffee is usually drank so strong as to injure children and grown persons of delicate constitution. All alcoholic drinks are dangerous, because they are so generally mixed with harmful matter, and because they so often lead to excess, and then to ruin. The common-sense maxim is, when there is danger, choose the safest course. The Christian maxim is, "We that are strong ought to bear the infirmities of the weak, and not to please ourselves."

Obedience to these two maxims would save thousands of young children and delicate persons from following the dangerous example of those "that are strong."

To make Tea.—The safest tea is the black, as less stimulating than green; both excite the brain and nerves when strong. The chief direction is to have water *boiling* hot. First soak the tea in a very little hot water, and then add boiling water.

To make Coffee.—Roast it slowly in a tight vessel, and so it can be stirred often. To roast all equally a dark brown and have none burnt, is the main thing. Keep it in a tight box, or, better, grind it fresh when used. Clear it by putting into it, when making, a fresh egg-shell crushed, or the white of an egg, or a small bit of fish-skin. Some filter, and some boil; and there are coffee-pots made for each method, and some that require nothing put in to clear the coffee. The aroma is retained just in proportion as the coffee is confined, both before making and also while making.

Fish-skin for Coffee.—Take it from codfish before cooking; have it nice and dry. Cut in inch squares, and take one for two quarts of coffee.

Cocoa.—The cracked is best. Put two table spoonfuls of it into three pints of cold water. Boil an hour for first use, save the remnants and boil it again, as it is very strong. Do this several times. For ground cocoa use two table-spoonfuls to a quart, and boil half an hour. Boil the milk by itself and add it liberally when taken up. For the *shells* of cocoa, use a heaping tea-cupful for a quart of water. Put them in over night and boil a long time.

Cream for Coffee and Tea.—Heat new milk and let it stand till cool and all the cream rises; this is the best way for common use. To every pint of this add pound and a quarter of loaf-sugar, and it will keep good a month or more, if corked tight in glass.

Chocolate.—Put three table-spoonfuls when scraped to each pint, boil half an hour, and add boiled milk when used.

Delicious Milk-Lemonade.—Half a pint of sherry wine and as much lemon-juice, six ounces loaf-sugar, and a pint of water poured in when boiling. Add not quite a pint of cold milk, and strain the whole.

Strawberry and Raspberry Vinegar.—Mix four pounds of the fruit with three quarts of cider or wine vinegar, and let them stand three days. Drain the vinegar through a jelly-bag and add four more pounds of fruit, and in three days do the same. Then strain out the vinegar for summer drinks, effervescing with soda or only with water.

White Tea, and Boys' Coffee, for Children.—Children never love tea and coffee till they are trained to it. They always like these drinks. Put two tea-spoonfuls of sugar to half a cup of hot water, and add as much good milk. Or crumb toast or dry bread into a bowl with plenty of sugar, and add half milk to half boiling water.

Dangerous Use of Milk.—Milk is not only drink, but rich food. It therefore should not be used as drink with other food, as is water or tea and coffee. Persons often cause bilious difficulties by using milk in addition to ordinary food as the chief drink. It is a well-established fact that some grown persons as well as young children can not drink milk, and in some cases can not eat bread wet with milk without trouble from it.

Simple Drinks.—Pour boiling water on mashed cranberries, or grated apples, or tamarinds, or mashed currants or raspberries; pour off the water, sweeten, and in summer cool with ice.

Pour boiling water on to bread toasted quite brown, or on to pounded parched corn, boil a minute, strain, and add sugar and cream, or milk.

Simple Wine Whey.—Mix equal quantities of milk and boiling water, add wine and sweeten.

Toast and Cider.—Take one third brisk cider and two thirds cold water, sweeten it, crumb in toasted bread, and grate on a little nutmeg. Acid jelly will do when cider is not at hand.

Panada.—Toast two or three crackers, pour on boiling water and let it simmer two or three minutes, add a well-beaten egg, sweeten and flavor with nutmeg.

Water Gruel.—Scald half a tumblerful of fresh ground corn-meal, add a table-spoonful of flour made into a paste, boil twenty minutes or more, and add salt, sugar, and nutmeg. Oat-meal gruel is excellent made thus.

Beef-Tea.—Pepper and salt some good beef cut into small pieces, pour on boiling water and steep half an hour. A better way is to put the meat thus prepared into a bottle kept in boiling water for four or five hours.

Tomato Syrup.—Put a pound of sugar to a quart of juice, bottle it and use for a beverage with water.

Sassafras Jelly.—Soak the pith of sassafras till a jelly, and add a little sugar.

Egg Tea, Egg Coffee, and Egg Milk.—Beat the yelk of an egg in some sugar and a little salt; add either cold tea or coffee or milk. Then beat the whites to a stiff froth and add. Flavor the milk with wine. Some do not like the taste of raw egg, and so the other articles may first be made boiling hot before the white is put in.

Oat-Meal Gruel.—Four table-spoonfuls of *grits*, (unbolted oat-meal,) a pinch of salt and a pint of boiling water. Skim, sweeten, and flavor. Or make a thin batter of fine oat-meal, and pour into boiling water; then sweeten and flavor it.

Pearl Barley-Water.—Boil two and a half ounces of pearl barley ten minutes in half a pint of water, strain it, add a quart of boiling water, boil it down to half the quantity, strain, sweeten, and flavor with sliced lemon or nutmeg.

Cream Tartar Beverage.—Put two even tea-spoonfuls cream tartar, to a pint of boiling water, sweeten and flavor with lemon-peel.

Rennet Whey, (good for a weak stomach after severe illness.)—Soak rennet two inches square one hour, add half a gill of water and a pinch of salt; then pour it into a pint of warm (not hot) milk. Let it stand half an hour, then cut it, and after an hour drain off the liquid. Let it stand awhile and drain off more whey.

Refreshing Drink for a Fever.—Mix sprigs of sage, balm, and sorrel with half a sliced lemon, skin on. Pour on boiling water, sweeten and cork it.

Food, etc., for an Infant.—Nothing is so good as cow's milk diluted and made only as sweet as mother's milk. Add less water as the infant grows older. Use milk from the same cow, as mixed milk is not so good. If the child's bowels are too loose, wait a little; if this continues, use boiled milk or rice-water. If constipated, a little magnesia may first be tried, and if it fails, call a doctor.

No other food is so good for an infant, if it is a healthy one, as milk. If it is not, the physician, and not an uneducated person, should direct.

Boiled rice and rice-water are highly recommended by physicians for convalescents and children with summer complaints.

Rubbing the body with the hand of a strong and healthy person is a great help in curing *disease* and restoring strength.

Many children as well as adults are sick from over-eating, causing biliousness, disordered stomachs, and headaches. The safest and best remedy is, *total abstinence from food* for a, day or more, giving the clogged organs a chance to throw off the excess.

Constipation is best cured by *loose dress,* exercise in fresh air, *sleeping warm* with a window open, and relief from exercise, care, or labor, and especially by a *daily* towel-bath, which in cold weather should be taken by a fire, especially by aged or delicate persons.

American gelatine in cholera infantum is better than farinaceous food.

Keep a sick-room quiet, neat, orderly, and well ventilated. Change the garment next the skin and the bed often. Ventilate a sick-room not by large openings, but by a half-inch crack at the top of one window and at the bottom of another. An open fire is a sure mode of ventilation.